ROY BROOKS was an eminent estate agent who became a national figure, mostly for one endearing reason; because of the puckish delight he took in telling the truth, the whole truth – and even the unwholesome truth. In a trade well-known for its euphemisms, optimistic clichés and skilful literary camouflage, he won the delighted applause of the property buying, and advertisement reading public – and the disapproving frowns of the conventional world of estate agents.

He was, too, a voice that spoke with the spirit of the sixties, which was when I first met him, in a television studio. Indeed, how could the newly muscled world of television debate not rush towards a man who casually and frequently commented, in current affairs discussions about housing and politics: "Houses are only mud and straw. They're often jerry built, usually overpriced and invariably falsely described." This from a man who, although he earned his living selling houses, believed that people preferred the unvarnished facts. He became a 'find' a 'television personality' and – more important – a spokesman for many a cause and always an advocate for the value of truth.

We became good friends and met, almost as frequently as professionals on television, during early Man Alive debates. What's more, I bought a house through him and he sold one for me. I cherish the scathing advertisement he used, then, to describe what I had always thought a pleasant bar in the corner of the sitting room and what he called "a white painted brick feature for holding exotic drinks, rather theatrical and in keeping with the pretentious style of the owner."

He died in 1971 and left behind an extraordinary collection of advertisements. His honesty and impudent originality were, surprisingly perhaps, rarely offensive. He walked his editorial tightrope with a natural flair and disarming humour. He espoused causes, advocated charities and benefited both. He brought a nationwide following to the Sunday Times and Observer and readers, who seemed no less attracted to his political and social homilies than to his scathing and acid descriptions of property. His really was a voice and a style that characterised – for me at least – the spirit of the Sixties.

Now, Tony Halstead and Colin Lowman, who were his two partners, have published some of the best of those advertisements in the well-founded belief that they will be as popular now as they were in those days. It may also remind us that much of his political comment is as relevant now as it was then and we can be reminded, too, what great response his appeals for help used to bring, and how many people were housed or looked after as a result.

This is, therefore, not only a book to remind and amuse but one that can take us back to a time when houses in London were a little less expensive . . . .

DESMOND WILCOX 22nd January 1985

"I WAS A TEENAGE LITERARY AGENT," confessed Mrs. L gazing thro' a wall of glass in her new Nursery/Study at the garden. *"A pity we had to cut the walnut tree down, . . ."* The rest is XVIIITH CENT. A small house of alleged Royal ownership in days of KEW PALACE. On KEW GREEN &, at rear, looking to river o'er tennis courts. A enchanting dble. drawing rm., Mod. kit. 2 principal bedrms., small 3rd bedrm for child or dwarf lodger. Bid. mod. bathrm. All the class of living behind a Georgian fanlight for less than the price of a suburban villa: ONLY £8,995 FREEHOLD.

FASHIONABLE CHELSEA, Lamont Rd. Do not be misled by the trim exterior of this modest Period Res. with its dirty broken windows; all is not well with the inside. The decor of the 9 rooms, some of which hangs inelegantly from the walls, is revolting. Not entirely devoid of plumbing, there is a pathetic kitchen & 1 cold tap. No bathrm., of course, but Chelsea has excellent public baths. Rain sadly drips through the ceiling on to the oilcloth. The pock-marked basement flr. indicates a thriving community of woodworm; otherwise there is not much wrong with the property. In the tiny back garden an Anderson shelter squats waiting. . . . Lse. 40 yrs? G.R. £50. SACRIFICE £6,750.

CHESTER SQ. BELGRAVIA. Under its mantle of dust & dirt this is a very fine house; there is even an air of aristocratic decay about the broken passenger lift. *"I'm afraid the lift is out of order we'll have to walk up . . ."* cannot fail to impress your guests. 5 principal bedrms., 2 staff rms., plus 3 attic rms., magnificent, vast "L" shaped 1st flr. drawing rm., about 35 ft., fine large dining rm., solid mahogany doors, study, a frightful old kit., 3 old fashioned bathrms. I suspect that under the grime, this eminent Banker's house is pretty sound; but better get a good surveyor. LONG 41 yr. lse. G.R. ONLY £100 p.a. Say, £19,995 but try any offer; owner might take a low price from deserving, but impecunious, young couple. Viewing Sunday 3–5. Knock 4 times.

LADY B WRITES: *"I want future home; somewhere like Norfolk, spacious, rambling, dilapidated – needing care (derelict if 2 rooms habitable) ... ready to take in young nieces and nephews from Africa when the upheaval is sparked off."* Unexpected disasters are bad enough, but avoidable ones even worse. Effective, full blooded sanctions that are carried out against Rhodesia/S. Africa, whatever the cost, are cheaper than the loss of a single life of either colour – but I'm no expert – just prefer people alive rather than dead – politically free rather than imprisoned. I suggest you all send ten bob, one year's sub to ANTI-APARTHEID NEWS, 89 Charlotte St. W1. ROY BROOKS.

FASHIONABLE CHELSEA. Fine 8 rm. house. 2 bathrms. Consent to let rms. (Estimated income £1,500 p.a. plus owner's suite; 3 gd. rms.) £3,000 spent bringing up to her own high standards by friend of Royalty. (Trekked 800 miles on horseback with 100 bearers & baby brother in meat safe to make African camp for Edward, Prince of Wales, & took *"elevenses"* – stewed duck served in chamberpot, with Great Queen Magui, aged 102: 13 husbands – 2 thrown by herself to the crocodiles, & who had tin of sardines & Golden Syrup on the table to show how English she was ...) Lse. 10 yrs. Thought renewable. G.R. only £20 p.a. £7,995, try ANY offer.

OPULENT 18TH CENTURY SETTING, FASHIONABLE ISLINGTON. NEWLY BUILT SUNNY 2nd. floor LUX. FLAT looking out over the lovely ancient trees and remnants of the aboriginal inhabitants quietly fishing in the canal which peacefully meanders through tended gardens of the well-preserved well-heeled intellectuals' neighbouring properties. BALCONY. 25ft. drawing rm, 2 bedrms., 2 mod. bathrms. Well fit. kit. Lse. 90 yrs. G.R. £45. £8,500 even try offer.

FASHIONABLE CHELSEA. Immaculate (protected) period res. of Colonel – late Heavy Foot & winner of Beau Brummel award (now framed in the downstairs lav.) shifting his moorings to be nearer his yacht. A superb 26ft L-drawing rm., sun pours in: windows both ends. Richly comfortable dining rm.; the elegant decor setting off paintings & scale model of his Folkboat which is owned with all the panache of a 12 metre. An air of exquisite refinement broods over the splendid master bedrooms., 2 other good bedrms., mod. bathrm. shower. One of the best kitchens I've seen. Maritime decor, of course. Gleaming parquet. Delightful little garden. Good parking in this little cul-de-sac. Good lse. G.R. ONLY £23.15 p.a. SACRIFICE £9,850. Even try ANY offer.

SCOTT OF THE GUARDIAN asks us to sell his elegant & historic George II, circa 1759. residence in CHEYNE WALK, CHELSEA: an address that immediately stamps you as a person of wealth & even – by sympathetic magic – of culture. A few doors from TURNER'S house, that fellow who always got home after a night on the loose, by sticking a fiver in the heel of his sock, to paint those magnificent sunsets. You've the same superb river view. Suitably magnificent 30 ft. dble. drawing rm., dining rm., study or 6th bedrm., 5 dble. bedrms., mod bathrm., well fit kit. Decor in impeccable taste. BARGAIN £27,750 FREEHOLD.

IT WAS NICE OF THE FOR-TUNATELY INDESTRUCTIBLE MR. STIRLING MOSS to make a generous reference to us apropos his Nassau house in last week's **SUNDAY TIMES**: but I do hope this will not bring a spate of outlandish properties like the disused light-house off the Irish coast etc. etc. **ALAS** it is **ONLY IN THE LONDON AREA** that we can, & will, sell or let anything. **ROY BROOKS**.

SPAN FLAT, FASHIONABLE BLACK-HEATH. At a gathering of distinguished architects which I had the pleasure of addressing the other night, another speaker, a Mr. Lyons, spoke most highly of the SPAN development &, with the aid of beautiful colour slides, convinced me, at least, that here were homes fit for the merito-cracy. (A local resident told me she was sure her neighbour was a surgeon as *"He came home with blood on his boots ...."*). Sunny grnd. flr. access to immac. landscaped garden. Lovely spacious drawing rm., 2 be-drms., fit. wdrbs., mod. bathrm., bkfastrm.-kit. Decor v. gd. Lse. 993 yrs. G.R. ONLY £20. GARAGE £30 p.a. A GIFT AT £3,990.

CHILDREN'S SURGEON, joining the Freemasons & going into the City, as a sort of medical missionary, to tend sick business men (*"Poor Dr. Faustus,"* said a wise old doctor friend of mine, and one of them; *"a millionaire at 40 – & dead at 42"*). Anyway, MUST SACRIFICE rather grand MOCK GEORGIAN det. SUTTON house. 5 bedrms., 4 big. 1 only just makes the grade as a bedrm., bathrm., principal lav. with throne in green brocade, lounge hall, drawing rm. which can be opened into dining rm. (32ft.) for entertaining, b'fast rm., lab.-sav. kit. 52 power points. BIG GARAGE. BIG GARDEN with fountain & fish pond – sadly depleted, however, by patients of nearby veterinary surgeon. Country air. 29 mins. Victoria. £8,995 FREEHOLD.

FLAT, Imposing 29ft drawing rm., dining rm. or 4th bedrm. 3 other gd. bedrms., 2 mod. bathrms. Steeped in culture – fellow tenants inc. famous playwright, an Air Marshal, 2 leading novelists & an OBE. The owner's wife is herself a prize winning Romantic Novelist ("You get high marks for chastity" said the judge.) A 10 yr. lse. for ONLY £2,850 – equal to ONLY £285 p.a.! Peppercorn rent.

MUSCLE MAN, weight-lifting champion & photographer of pin-ups offers his elegant little top flr. (7th) FLAT. FASHIONABLE ST. JOHN'S WOOD. Drawing rm., balcony, dble. bedrm. tiled bathrm., mod. kit. LIFT. Perfect: quiet & sunny. Baby forces move. Lse. 5 yrs. ONLY £420 p.a. low offer f. & f.

SEMI-GLOSSY MAG. EDITOR, WRITER & WORLD RANGING V.I.P. JOURNALIST (He has even had an invitation to Buckingham Palace – marked " Tradesman's Entrance") offers his new ('58) house, which, with resident poodle (*" Reluctant to leave"*) much photographed for Ads. with real artificial flowers stuck in front garden. Sparkling all white decor, spacious drawing rm., abt. 24ft. Dining alcove. Well fit. kit., big larder, 3 decent bedrms., mod. tiled bathroom. GARAGE. Some of the most refined neighbours in LAMBETH, within earshot of Big Ben, walking distance of House of Commons & hard by an all night launderette. Small back gdn., lawn & cherry tree – all this for a mere £4,995, even try offer.

Lse. 995 yrs. G.R. Only 8 gns.

THANKS FOR LETTERS with details. I've passed on £100 to Save the Children Fund who write *"Many small children, hideously burned, look like little red skeletons. Their eyes alone indicate that they are alive. At present they are placed in the care of their families immediately after leaving the operating theatre."* This fund urgently needs *"Grace & Favour"* shop to sell Christmas cards. I'm investigating other direct aid to pass on further amounts. One told me Americans are embarrassed & slightly obstructive about their little victims. As Ky their much loved *"Meaningful"* S. Vietnam protégé is an open admirer of A. HITLER, why don't they set up Gas & Incinerator Chambers as a final solution. The original manufacturers are still in business in Germany. ROY BROOKS.

N.10. CLOSE HIGHGATE WOODS. The Edwardian abode of Gentleman Lecturer on Psychology & Lady Child Psychologist. The children of this union *"Climb over the fence, gambol on the grass & pick pounds of blackberries – can't see a house: in summer you have"* she says, *"the illusion of living in the country."* Ent. Hall, comfortable drawing rm., dining rm. semi open plan to well fit kit. 4 bedrms., mod. bathrm. FREEHOLD £7,495.

DISTINGUISHED LIBERAL S. AF-RICAN POLITICAL SCIENTIST & wife: former sec. S. African Liberal Party. *"My country needs me – later ..."* In the meantime he's going to Welsh University. *"I can handle Africaans – I think I can cope with the language ..."* & must sacrifice LUX. MEWS COTTAGE nr. FASHIONABLE QUEEN'S CLUB. 2 dble. bedrms. spacious drawing rm. which makes admirable library & study, lux. b & k. GARAGE. Lease 5½ yrs. Rent £400 p.a. v. mod. fig. to include f. & f.

£4,995 FREEHOLD. The Smooting, mod. architect blt. (circa 1954) res. of OLIVER, the Cambridge scientist son of my old friend the late TOM WINTRINGHAM, the " English Captain" who found Franco in Spain. 3 bedrms., one as study which, poised on the rim of KNAPP HILL nr. Woking, commands a rather splendid vista to the distant wooded hills. Pleasant booklined sitting rm., dining rm. with French window to garden, with flowers and sandpit and nice inaccessible jungly bit at end. Mod. b & k. *"Outside"* says wife, a Viking lady, *"It's very English – leaded lights. Inside"* she adds, peering thro' the Venetian blinds, *"it's very Danish ..."*

SURGEON'S FLAT in fashionable (1958) neo-Georgian block where persons of title mingle democratically with the medicos. Home of brilliant BRUDENELL THE KNIFE (obtainable in stainless steel, double bladed and equally adaptable for icing the cake – or biopsy). With delightful disregard for cash he's refused to patent it; in the interest of humanity. Lots of sun & near Heath. 3 DBLE. bedrms., drawing rm., mod. tiled bathrm., large kit. Lovely gardens. GARAGE. Blackheath's loss is Bradford's gain – he's going to the Paris of the north & MUST SELL. ONLY £4,950. Lse. 98 yrs. G.R. ONLY £18.

ST. PETER'S VILLAS, ST. PETER'S SQ., W.8. An address which places you among the creme de la creme. Stricken by the freeze & *"Govt's broken promise to us"* (Like many other doctors he's still running his old Mk. VI – it's the spivs & pop singers who can afford the S.3's) our client MUST SELL enchanting REGENCY HOUSE. Thousands spent, original Adam features. Super dble. drawing rm. Cosy dining rm. Study or 4th dble. bedrm. 3 other bedrms. mod. bathrm. super kit. **£14,995 FREEHOLD.**

TO SHOW there is another point of view about Vietnam I reproduce a letter received this week. ROY BROOKS. *"Sir, I have complained about your scurrilous attack on the Americans and for that matter the Germans to The Observer, the Advertising Association and the Press Council. I think you are making a mistake – you are advertising houses that are not the public conscience of Britain – or, as you seem to image, of the world."* Yr. fly. (signed) Mrs. de la Mabotiere, London N.W.3.

SOLICITOR, respected editor of Legal Periodical & restless girl model forced to leave their ISLAND PARADISE at THAMES DITTON & interesting neighbours "Coming back from the Swan" he says, *"Strangers in the night like the lady carrying her clothes in a bundle & muttering how it all began in the Scampi bar . . . ."* 60ft. RIVER FRONTAGE & o'lking Hampton Court Park. Delightful 26ft. dble. drawing rm., fine kit. dining rm., 3 dble. bedrms., lux. bathrm. Delightful garden, immaculate throughout. Lse. 95 yrs. G.R. £30 p.a. £7,995.

GURTH KING HAROLD'S KID BROTHER – heavily armoured in brass curtain rings (B.B.C. 2.) Offers his elegant, fashionable CHELSEA 1st flr. FLAT so spacious, you can isolate the guests. Delightful 23ft. drawing rm. French windows to balcony. Unusual dining rm. divided to make 4th bedrm. Mod. bath. & kit. Decor gd. Lse. 31½ yrs. G.R. ONLY £50. £9,995.

WESTMINSTER ABBEY CHOIR BOY AT QUEEN'S WEDDING sits at piano thinking of his next pop number. Gracious drawing rm., which might be in a rich country rectory, bucolic outlook over CLAPHAM COMMON. Exquisite dble. bedrm., a simulacrum of a medieval tent richly coloured drapes to wall & ceiling. Housekeepers bedrm., lux. coloured bathrm & kit. £28 per week income from Dr. in base. & refined bedsitters upstairs. £9,995 FREEHOLD.

RETURNING TO CANADA. Film Director and little shepherdess from The Roman Spring of Mrs. Stone, sacrifice for immediate sale, this solid PUTNEY bourgeois family res. which they have transformed into what she describes as *"A pretentious little house."* Complete with NEW OIL CENTRAL HEATING and bathrm. in the American taste; new tub, Beardsleys on the wall, black curtains and a chandelier (also, of course, a chandelier in the w.c. – and room for 2nd bathrm.). A gorgeous BIG drawing rm., fine dining rm., 5th bedrm. or Montage rm., b'fast rm. new kit., 4 perfect bedrms. The principal bedrm. is a splendid 25ft. affair in ersatz Adam style. Interesting garden. £6,990 FREEHOLD.

FASHIONABLE DULWICH. Dr. must quickly sell new (59) SUPER-LUX. Architect blt. RES. as wife taken to Action Painting – keeps introducing new materials – earth, sand ... Elegant 30ft. drawing rm, pol. wd. flr. delightful b'fastrm./kit. 3 fine bedrms. one to balcony, lux. tiled bathrm. GARAGE. Gdn. apple & pears, roses. ONLY £6,550.

NEW ('58) ARCHITECT MOD. LUX. CONTEMPORARY HOUSE. High, sunny & healthy. Forest Hill, DULWICH COLLEGE ESTATE. Highlander (ex. bombaimer) & wife (ex Roedean) write: *"Hidden persuader, left rat-race for Academic post: going Nth ... I can fly, film hypnotise ..."* OVERLKG PARKLAND & priv. access to WOODED HILL behind: abt 10 mins. VICTORIA. Superb spacious 1st flr. drawing rm., dining rm. to patio. 3 gd. bedrms, lux b & k. Utility rm. gd. garden. GARAGE. Featured in Glossy mags. Lse. 95 yrs. G.R. £20. ONLY £5,550 even try offer.

THANKS TO READERS WHO WROTE *"Congratulations on verdict of Press Council ... trust that they (The Observer) nor you will be intimidated by the kind of people who make the complaint. – Mrs. K."* Apropos my ad: *"Americans are embarrassed and slightly obstructive about their little victims. As Ky their 'much loved meaningful South Vietnam Protégé is an open admirer of A. HITLER, why don't they set up Gas and Incinerator Chambers as a final solution, the original manufacturers are still in business in Germany."* More constructive I should have thought than Mr. D. Astor's comments to the Press Council: *"Mr. Brooks's political utterances were often so far-fetched as to be self-defeating."* Complacency is out of place. At least *"my"* remarks have resulted in my being able to pass on cash and caramison to several units succouring the innocent child victims of American aggression – Condemned by all Christians left of Billy Graham. ROY BROOKS.

"THEY DRANK THE GAY BUBBLY IN ECCLESTON SQ." Wrote SAKI in 1912 in his novel of English upper-class collaborators prophesying German aggression. A RATHER SPLENDID PENTHOUSE in this noble garden sq. with TENNIS. Spacious drawing rm., picture window sliding back to sunbathing terrace; principal dble. bedrm., 5ft × 6ft. Pygmy bedrm.; the only snag: *"access only through our bedrm."* says top Ad. man who did those wonderful Army recruiting ads., as well as being against The Bomb, now turned Anthropologist. Lease 86 yrs. G.R. £80 p.a. Only £4,400.

JAMES DUFUS OF DALCLAVER-HOUSE, gentleman, offers his elegant 3rd. flr. CHEYNE ROW CHELSEA FLAT, which has gone up in the world since CARLYLE, opposite, complained of his neighbours' chickens. Drawing rm. of great dignity with electric lights points for family portraits, which can be obtained in the Fulham or King's Rd. 2 bedrms. fit. wardrobe for kilts, mod. b. & k. Lse. 95 yrs. G.R. ONLY £50. £5,550 TRY OFFER. Little enough for an address that sets you apart from the common herd.

£5,750 FHLD. *"I bought this house off Wandsworth Common for its quiet solidity, warmth & comfort. 15 mins. Town,"* said client from Th' North who has spent £2,000 on restoring this double fronted semi. to its Victorian prime. *"To house my Victorian treasures . . . . have to entertain a lot of foreigners, like to show them British way of life. I'm Chairman of the Conservative Party . . . . . Still play cricket . . . There's a fine bust of Wellington on the landing . . ."* Commodious & comfortable drawing rm., gd. dining rm., smoking rm. or 5th bedrm., 4 dble. bedrms., fit. wdrbs., 1 basin, new b. & k. Garden.

HAMPSTEAD N.W.3. Off fashionable Redington Rd. which leads to Heath. Ent. flr. mais. of one who, like the client above, is also in advertising. A Radical, with more contemporary decor, he seemed to agree with my view that the best consumer protection would be to frank every article with the manufacturer's production price. On hillside, so all principal rms. above ground. Attractive drawing rm., principal dble. bedrm., bathrm., decent b'fast rm., kit. LEISURE UNIT, PLUS Dwarf's suite. Tiny "bedrm." 7ft. × 8ft. suit small country's Diplomat. Tiny garden. Lse. to Xmas 1996. G.R. ONLY £50 ONLY £3,500.

WELL KNOWN DR. & OSTEOPATH'S BEAUTIFUL BECKENHAM lux. postwar family res. secluded ½ acre backing parkland; own swimming pool 6 bedrms., mod. bathrm., 3 reception rms., English Rose kit. OAK FLOORS. Dble. car port. Huge conservatory for Balls, nectarines, grapes etc. £4,000 spent gilding the lily: whoever buys this will doubtless become Beckenham's First Citizen for a modest £11,250 FREEHOLD.

BENEVOLENT BAVARIAN BARON (R.C. & did not help Hitler – he was 10 at the time) & former model, sedulously seek simple 3-rm. flat within reach of the Tube. ROY BROOKS.

A FACE FROM THE PAST; now minus its beard, reminds me of my distinguished client's original letter some years ago; *"It was pointed out to me that it would be a Good Thing to buy and convert a big house into flats. It has been a good thing for my Architect, Surveyor, Builder, Accountant, Solicitor ..."* He shld. have consulted us earlier: the poor fellow made a modest loss. ANYWAY he's now offered us a fine ENT. FLR. (Up steps like 1st flr.) SUNNY HAMPSTEAD FLAT, Imposing 29ft drawing rm., dining rm. or 4th bedrm. 3 other gd. bedrms., 2 mod. bathrms. Steeped in culture – fellow tenants inc. famous playwright, an Air Marshal, 2 leading novelists & an OBE. The owner's wife is herself a prize winning romantic Novelist (*"You get high marks for chastity"*) said the judge.) A 10 yr. lse. for ONLY £2,850 – equal to ONLY £285 p.a.! Peppercorn rent.

DEVOUT SOCIALIST SOLICITOR & S. AFRICAN GIRL NATIONALIST sadly eschew the rich luxury of their sparkling, mod. Maida Vale PENTHOUSE STUDIO FLAT. Gorgeous Studio drawing rm. with gallery has 20ft. window! Sunbathing roof gdn. for open air lovers. 2 bedrms., lux. tiled bathrm., super fit. kit. exquisite decor. CENTRAL HEATING. C.H.W. LIFT – THE LOT. Suit film star or Solicitor who has done well in the property market. Lse. 7 yrs. ONLY £400 p.a. SACRIFICE FAR BELOW COST.

EDGE HILL, WIMBLEDON, high & not far Common, nr. FASHIONABLE R.C. Church The Lux. newly blt. (3 yrs. ago) 1st & 2nd flr. mais. of lady missionary to darkest PERU & other parts of S. America who, like me, thinks that the spread of literacy & food & – by small doses – of interdenominational simple Christian principles, is more import-ant than even space tely. Lovely 22ft. drawing rm., 2 gd. bedrms., tiled bathrm., well fit. kit. Decor only fair. GARAGE. ONLY £4,995. Lse. 97 yrs. G.R. ONLY £20.

THE SPLENDID HYDE PARK SUNNY 3rd flr. flat (lift) of failed Theatri-cal Designer, kitchen operative & opulent collector of bois clair furniture. Impressive entrance hall, 2 LARGE reception rms., 2 dble. bedrms., 2 bathrms., 1 super new lux. shower, vanitory unit & extensive wall mir-rors, American kit. super ckr. & spit. Pres. lse. to Sept 1975, abt. £550 p.a. Mod. fig. val. f & f.

EMPIRE BUILDER (*"I left after my fri-end put Independence Badge which Tanganyi-kan Govt. issued on his dog's collar ..."*) GOING S. AFRICA & MUST SELL *"Mawingo"* New architect blt. '64. *"Visi-tors"*, he says, *"are awed by its beauty & luxury."* BEAUTIFUL BICKLEY, 12 miles TOWN. In beautiful EASY garden. *"Planted nothing that won't stand up for itself."* Gor-geous 23ft drawing rm. dining rm., study, 4 DBLE. bedrms., 2 lux. bathrms., SHOW-ERS. Gold fits. Super Kit. Dble. GARAGE. worth over £20,000. He'll consider any offer on £15,500 FREEHOLD as he's yearning for Sun & Freedom.

ANYBODY WHO IS ANYBODY SEEMS TO FOLLOW THIS COLUMN (*"We always like to read a good paper in prison,"* said an ex-convict to me recently *"following the property market keeps us in touch ..."*) Anyway we have thousands & thousands of unsatisfied applicants for whom we need HOUSES AND FLATS in GREATER LONDON. ROY BROOKS.

WILL ANYONE TAKE PITY ON A NASTY OLD HOUSE adj. REGENT'S PK. TER. On still nights the friendly howl of the Hyaena floats over the Mappin terraces & one can, maybe, imagine oneself far away from our acquisitive society. 9 rms., 2 bathrms., kit. All in pretty foul order. Will only sell for single occupancy to gentlepeople. G.R. £70. Lse. abt. 75 yrs. £7,250 (I expect we'll see it resold, done up, in a year or so for abt. £14,000).

FASHIONABLE HAMPSTEAD, N.W.3. Sunny 1st. flr. FLAT. Airy Drawing rm. 2 DOUBLE bedrms. well fit. kit. Bathrm. where Chartered Accountant and American wife brew beer in the bath *"like her dad did in San Francisco – except he made Gin ..."* Lse. 39 yrs. G.R. ONLY £25 p.a. ONLY £5,750 & try any offer.

FASHIONABLE BLACKHEATH. Lux. rew. blt. (1956) in a reverent XVIIIth cent. manner by a Mr. Brown the architect who did up the Paragon – where this is. Mile of vista of Heath & Park. A shrine of objets d'art: a frying pan painted by Wm. Scott over the genuine reproduction mantelpiece in the 24ft. Drawing rm., 2 decent bedrms., super b. & k. Decor: a conception of childless couple (no dirty paw marks) who, after he chucked in a promising career as a civil service clerk for (*"Abstract landscapes – you can see the earth and sky ...."* no danger of them being hung upside down. REB) is moving to great affluence & MUST SACRIFICE 77 yr. lse. G.R. £20 for £7,550.

FASHIONABLE HIGHGATE. Rich Tycoon eschews family business for abstract Art & St. Ives (this one said it didn't matter which way up his pictures were hung – & why not? After all a pretty woman looks just as good upside down.) Circa '04: it's got an ugly face but lovely light big rooms inside. NONBASE RESIDENCE. Split-level double drawing rm., abt. 30ft., study or extra bedrm., gd. dining rm., 5 gd. bedrms, fine new kit., tiled bathrm. with shower. 3ft. double STUDIO with large top light. £8950 FREEHOLD, even try offer.

OFF FASHIONABLE HOLLAND PARK AVENUE. Alleged development area. PERIOD RESIDENCE modernised 10 yrs. ago for the Ban the Bomb Cellist Joy Waller (*"bit squarer though than my musical namesake"*) Big dble. drawing rm., 3 gd. bedrms., b & k. plus *"rear"* good sized STUDIO – door to Pottery Lane. Decor not too bad as you enter: gets worse as you go up. £4,995 FREEHOLD.

LITTLE VENICE. Not only fashionable but, judging by the neighbours, a veritable compost heap of culture. Sunny 1st flr. mais. overlkg. beautiful gardens; haunt of wild birds. Gracious 24ft. × 18ft. drawing rm., big 18 × 18ft. dining rm., 3 best bedrms., attic for servant &/or Master's study, b. & k. Lse. 9 yrs. ONLY £450 p.a.

WATES LUX. CORNER HOUSE. The drawing rm. has been thrown into dining rm. (sliding drs.) to cope with the mad whirl of entertaining that goes on in UPPER NORWOOD. 2 gd. bedrms. easily conv. to 3 bedrms., super b. & k. £5,750 FHLD.

YOUNG GIRL. A DEDICATED THEATRICAL writes: *"I want to get married. I have found a prospective husband but this seems to be a small issue as compared with the other greater one – i.e. where to put him."* She can afford about £6 per week and may be able to pay a small premium. ROY BROOKS.

SHE WAS ONLY A TEA-TASTER'S DAUGHTER who, passing through a remount depot, became a can-can dancer and dental receptionist and, finally came to roost in this FASHIONABLE CHELSEA SQ., and whose lovely home we are privileged to offer. DIVIDED as: ent. Flr. mais. – 2 dble. bedrms., 2 rec. opening into one gorgeous 35 ft. rm. for receptions, large bathrm., kit. Fit. carpets inc. Small garden. 1st flr. as STUDIO FLAT – own b. & k.-dining rm. Upper mais. – 2 dble. bedrms. large rec. rm., mod. b. & k.-dining rm. Pres. lse. to Aug. '73. ONLY £200 p.a. BARGAIN £5,990. HUGE INCOME POTENTIAL.

FASHIONABLE CHELSEA. Fashionable publisher, who has come a long way – via THE NAKED & THE DEAD, since he was employed as a scarecrow in a cherry orchard in '41, now moving to greater affluence, sacrifices small but impressive period style architect blt. ('57) res. Elegant drawing rm., 3 bedrms. The Master bedrm. is big, dble. & superb, the 2nd. O.K. in the 3rd. Mr. Andre Deutsch dares only accommodate the more dwarfish of his less successful writers but, he adds: *"Sunshine & warmth pour in & on a summer eve the street looks like a UTRILLO."* Lux. b. & k. Undeveloped garden. Space for extra rms. &/or GARAGE. Lse. to 1998. G.R. ONLY £45. BARGAIN £8,990

FASHIONABLE DULWICH VILLAGE. White painted family house. Quite a gracious drawing rm. French Windows to garden, now MUSIC RM. *"A piano; no: no tely – I'm lucky I only work on it."* says little EMERGENCY WARD 10 actress who, marrying Film Director must move. Dining rm., study or 5th bedrm., b'fast rm., 4 bedrms., b. & k. Hundreds recently spent. Lse. to 2004. G.R. £8. A gift at £4,550 even try offer.

£7,990 FREEHOLD TRY ANY OFFER. LAMBETH MANOR. S.E.1. 18th Cent. GEORGIAN HOUSE (in the family over 100 yrs. Grandpa bought it as he thought Waterloo Railway was going thro' it – but it doesn't. *"Titled neighbours in my childhood"* says present Chatelaine. Drawing rm. over 20ft., study, dining rm., 5 bedrms., b. & k. Garden with large fig tree. Original chimneypieces only need unblocking. A warm comfortable, shabby house.

REGENT'S PARK ROAD. Old Etonian's scruffy Period res. overlooking PRIMROSE HILL & ST. PAUL'S. Self-styled *"Rejected Poet & Painter."* (It's always possible to tell an English gentleman from the lesser breeds. The latter boast of their successes, the former speak only of their failures. Our distinguished client has attempted, unsuccessfully, to paint out his *"very nude mural"* in the hall, as a concession to middle class taste.) VAST 1st flr. 30ft. drawing rm., nice ceiling, balcony, gd. dining rm., new ground flr. kit. 4/5 bedrms., bathrm., extra kit. for genteel subletting. ONLY £13,990 FHLD.

APROPOS MY REFERENCE TO R.A.F. SQUADRONS we were unable to send to Singapore in last war, a reader writes blaming "The Socialists." For the record: in ~~1919~~ 1939 Socialists, like myself, in the Territorials tended to put part of the blame on, say, the £40 million lent to Hitler by British Tory Industrialists & Bankers up to 1931. ROY BROOKS.

WITH ALL THE THOROUGHNESS OF A TEUTON & NONE OF THE NASTINESS, PAUL HANSARD, the brilliant actor who found it expedient to leave Hitler's Berlin as a child in '34 has superbly modernised this FINE FASHIONABLE ISLINGTON PERIOD HOUSE in wide road of well cared for houses. A most elegant yet comfortable 25ft. double drawing rm. Good dining rm. kit. A study of peace & dignity or 3rd. bedrm. 2 other bedrms. Bathrm. DECOR EXCELLENT. Pleasant small garden, grass & snowdrops. ONLY £8,650 FREEHOLD.

BARNES COMMON, with 2 stations, Green line & other buses escape is easy from this quiet, respectable suburb. A well built EDWARDIAN FAMILY RES. 24ft. dble. drawing rm. 4 bedrms., (3 gd. but cheese shaped, the 4th would only comfortably accommodate a triangular door). Not a bad bathrm., kit. decor is a bit *"put-offing"* but in the doctors bedrm., hundred of books COMPLETELY lined the walls revealing only the mauve ceiling. Garage & garden with what the Dr. describes as *"the rather attractive back passage."* Terrific bargain ONLY £6,625 FREEHOLD.

HARDENED NAIL MAN, CITIZEN KANE, whose OBO tool sticks things on the wall without broken thumbs, sacrifices his SUPERB HAMPSTEAD SUNNY 2nd flr. FLAT with CENT. HEAT. Imposing main entrance, gleam. parquet & ascent upon a rich red carpet. Dining hall (the bar, mit awning, placed in the basement when baby came). Drawing rm., 2 bedrms., super mod. b & k., stainless steel Leisure unit. Secluded gdn. & absentee Landlord ("The nicest person imaginable") ONLY £360 p.a.

MR. WISHART (former member, he says, of BAND OF HOPE: & proud descendant of CALVINIST GEO. WISHART who was burnt at the stake at St. Andrews) has given up selling drugs & is going to Edinburgh to sell beer must sell NEW (60) LUX. HOUSE, on the site of ROYAL HUNTING FOREST. Dulwich College grant him access to a bit that's left at the bottom of his garden. ONLY 12 mins. London Bridge. Lovely 1st-flr. drawing rm. & dining rm. to super lab. sav. kit., 3 bedrms., NURSERY or 4th dble. bedrm., lux. bathrm., ONLY £5,550.

THE DOWER HOUSE, off QUEEN'S GATE, S. KEN. The now redundant Town res. of charming Colonel's Lady who left India & the Army with the passing of the horse for a quiet retirement: ARP & the London Blitz. 25ft. drawing rm. of great loftiness & beautiful polished floor. Large "L" dining rm. (space for extra bedrm.) 2 bedrms., Memsahib's bathrm. Extra bath in Kit. for servant or lodger. ONLY £12,990 FHLD.

NASH MASTERPIECE, PARK VILLAGE WEST. REGENT'S PK. One of the last bastions against Socialism. Describing himself as *"A frustrated young Tory"* (he is only 40 & arranges flowers for a living), our client tires of this lovely house on which he has lavished £4,000 in 2 years. Exquisite 25ft. withdrawing rm., parquet & a fine chimney-piece, elegant dining rm., 2 master bedrms. & marble bathrm. & marble lav., light base. has 2 good bedrms., bathrm. & kit. Top (2nd) flr. has gorgeous 32 × 24 ft. STUDIO, plus good sized model's disrobing rm. Used for Political parties. Crown Lse. 14 yrs. renewable. Only £220 p.a. £8,950.

**DO YOU WANT TO DISPOSE OF YOUR
HOUSE OR FLAT BEFORE THE BOT-
TOM DROPS OUT OF THE
MARKET?** Nothing is too humble for us
to handle, on the other hand we have a
number of upper class clients whose vast
resources make mortgage unneccessary.
ROY BROOKS.

**OCEAN RACER MUST SELL SMART
PRINCES GATE MEWS, S.W.7.** MEWS
COTTAGE with HUGE GARAGE which
takes his two cars and more. Charming 1st flr.
Drawing rm. Good dble. bedrm., Bathrm.,
super new kit. Immac. new decor. Living here
must be like being pressed between the pages
of JENNIFER'S DIARY – the nearest thing
to the plebs I have met in the Mews was a
charming Hohenzollern Princess who pro-
fessed Marxism. However, a middle class
buyer will probably be tolerantly accepted as
"Someone's chauffeur ..." Good lease: 10
yrs. extendable/ G.R. ONLY £25. A GIFT
AT £5,995.

FASHIONABLE CHELSEA, FAMOUS TITE ST., (Where O. Wilde, friend of FRANK HARRIS lived.) Quiet sunny, 3rd. flr. flat off CHEYNE WALK where client, an important theatrical producer of "dustbin" drama and middle class theatre, says he can actually see the river if someone holds his feet. 2 bedrms., elegant drawing rm., altho' in show-biz quiet good taste, no velvet flock wallpaper. A Bolan over fireplace. Mod. tiled bathrm., well fit. b'fast, rm., kit. clkrm., Gd. Lse. 5 yrs. Unrapacious Landlord. ONLY £475 p.a.

LUXURY MAYFAIR FLAT which Mrs. P. (a former Archer character who got out just in time before getting her fingers – inter alia – burnt to make a Roman holiday for the B.B.C. who out-horrify the emergent I.T.V.) describes as ravishingly beautiful, aloof (she means there's no lift. R.E.B.) French wallpapers, fabulous Louis XVI marble mantel, real coal fires altho' of course CENTRAL HEATING. Bathroom, an ablutionists dream – solid marble, gold taps to bidet. *"Char might stay...."* Forced move; sacrifice far, far below cost. Elegant drawing rm., 2 fine dble. bedrms, enchanting breakfast rm./kit. Spanish tiles around the double sinks. Lease until March 1977 at £410 p.a. rising in 1966 to £435 p.a. and in 1973 to £460 p.a?

FABULOUS BARGAIN. The Three Shields Gallery off KENSINGTON CHURCH ST. W.8. A dear little GEORGIAN HOUSE converted, in a prosperous shopping street, into thriving gallery (grnd. flr. showrm. & roomy basement, so dry, envelopes stored). 2 offices on 1st flr. or splendid dble. drawing rm. & 3 other gd. rms., b & k. Sells superior mod. pottery (*"nothing art & crafty"*) & the nicer sort of greetings card to an exclusive clientele. (My favourites *"Your face looks as though it's worn out two bodies"* & *"We are at home on Sundays between 5 & 7. Hope you are the same,"* are alas, not in stock.) It's more than a comfortable income – It's a way of life, of course, I suppose there's nothing to stop you turning it into a chopsuey joint, fish parlour or modern art gallery, & really coining the money. A BARGAIN, either to live in as a house or live on as a business: £12,990 FHLD. EVEN TRY OFFERS.

WE HAVE A RATHER REPULSIVE OLD MAN who, with his child wife, are looking for an elegant Town Res. Pref. BELGRAVIA, CHELSEA or S. KEN. Price not important but must be realistic as he has, at least, his head screwed on the right way. Usual scale commission required. ROY BROOKS.

HISTORIC MERTON ROAD S.W.18 near where Nelson played with Emma Hamilton. A fine Christian home (Mum rescues unwanted babies & daughter bans the bomb; the Church of England is less likely to fling you out for this than the Labour Party. R.E.B.) Spacious mid-Victorian house close to Southfields. 19ft. drawing rm., dining rm. to conservatory, large breakfast rm., 5 bedrms., (4 double) bathrm., kit. Good 80ft. rear garden with apples, pear & soft fruits. Parking space for car. In excellent order. Freehold £6,990.

"TOO BIG SINCE AU PAIR GIRL LEFT ..." says VOICE-OVER QUEEN – Central School of Speech & Drama's most famous graduate who does those Suet and pre-stressed corset ads on tely. The TOWN HOUSE which she and session drummer must sell, cross over Albert Bridge from Chelsea, is in *"Most respected street in BATTERSEA, by PARK."* Elegant 27ft dble. drawing rm., attractive large b'fast rm., super-fit wood panelled kit. 4 dble. bedrms. new lux. bathrm., study or 5th bedrm. Immac. throughout – thousands spent. Garden of herbs & flowers. £9,990 FHLD.

FASHIONABLE S. KEN. HARRINGTON GDNS. – laudably mentioned by A. J. ALAN. Only the horse is missing from Cavalry colonel's spacious upper mais. NO LIFT. The place, quiet & sunny, like a country house – crawling with saddles and the agreeable impedimenta of hippomania. Cent. Heat. Elegant 20ft. sq. drawing rm., 4 bedrms., mod. bathrm., family kit./b'fast rm. Lse. 97 yrs. G.R. £75 p.a. £10,990.

FASHIONABLE ROEHAMPTON VILLAGE. Venerable economist (formerly of the Times & girl actress/sculptress, SACRIFICE their converted & modernised COTTAGE RES. where sun (south aspect) shines down on them & the patio leading to turfed garden with mini fig tree. 2 best bedrms. small 3rd. bedrm. for child or dwarf. Drawing rm. & dining rm. Doors between exuberantly torn off to facilitate party flux. Bathrm. & kit. Terrific bargain £6,350 FREEHOLD.

FASHIONABLE   ISLINGTON. A vaguely ecclesiastical atmosphere broods over this scheduled-for-preservation GOTHIC REVIVAL GARDEN SQUARE. (I know Estate Agents have debased the meaning of *"Unique"* but our Mr. Halstead says it really is). In this 12 rm. res. of English speaking Australian Surgeon, 2 in the base. are rather sordid & top is attic but the rest are not bad if you discount the decor which is dirty, dark & depressing. Not entirely without plumbing, there is a cold tap around somewhere. Garden, heavily disguised under a patch of weeds. Client says house has a good survey. GREAT BARGAIN £7,850 FHLD. & try any, yes ANY OFFER.

AN AMERICAN LADY   sent a photostat of a horrifying letter from the firm who make the deathly Napalm Jelly in which they say it is *"Good citizenship to supply the Government with all it needs ..."* If the politicians & their compliant supporters were as efficient & intelligent as the medicos we could stop this bloody war. ROY BROOKS.

£2,400 TRY ANY OFFER, FASHIONABLE CHELSEA.   The Bohemian establishment of Smithson the famous architect – the originator, he claims, of THE NEW BRUTALISM. Now enriched and somewhat refined (he is remodelling Boodles). We have sold him something expensive in The Boltons. 24ft dble. drawing rm., grnd. flr. b'fast rm., kit., a terrible bathrm., but can also be used as bedrm., 4 other rms. including a strange *"house within a rm."* inhabited by advanced artist (Framed Barrow-boys *"grass"* embellished with lawn tennis white marker). Another kit. with shower-bath. Small squalid gdn. sprouting headed statues. Pres. lse. to March 65. G.R. ONLY £10.

SMART KINNERTON ST. KNIGHTS-BRIDGE COTTAGE WITH DOUBLE GARAGE of retired racing motorist (6½-litre green label Bentleys & hotted-up fire pumps) & girl actress who sadly leave their elegant, but slightly child-pocked home. Attractive drawing rm., dining rm. (poss. 4th bedrm.), 3 bedrms., bathrm., kit., stainless steel sink but nothing flash. Sun-baked flat roof. Gd. 27 yrs. lse. only £50 G.R. £8,995.

CARDIAC SURGEON & GIRL THEATRE NURSE gone North MUST SELL THEIR MOD. ('58) BLOCK FLAT. 1st. (TOP) flr. HEALTHY HENDON near superlative Park & almost too near Brent Station. 20 mins. Oxford St. Sunny, comfortable Drawing rm. 3 bedrms. Mod. bathrm. Good sized b'fastrm./kit. 12ft. sq. garden. Lse. 20 yrs. G.R. £12 ONLY £5,750.

£4,850 FREEHOLD. PASTORAL PINNER. Young couple's lovingly modernised EDWARDIAN COTTAGE HOME dedicated to his music (Operatic/Oratorio tenor) & her specimens. WONDERFUL 200 ft. garden, huge lawn secluded by Lilac, laburnam, apple & pear trees. Rhododendron, roses, milk, eggs etc. from Farm nearby. ONLY 23 mins. Baker St. Drawing rm. or Music rm., dining rm., b'fastrm./kit. 3 bedrms. mod. bathrm.

LIFE AT THE TOP OF PUTNEY HILL o'looking HEATH. In well tended grounds; the mode. LUX. BLOCK 1st. flr. FLAT of *"Socialist miner's son from the Welsh Valleys"* who has made good in Advertising. *"At Oxford got a 1st. in History – it helps – the logic y'know – promoted pink toilet soap on tely, filmed nude French model in her bath ..."* Ent. hall, drawing rm. PARQUET & door to balcony. 3 Bedrm., bathrm., well fit. kit. GARAGE. Lse. 93 yrs. GR ONLY £40. SACRIFICE £6,995.

LAWN CRES. KEW. Oddly enough it really does overlook a lawn, surrounded by trees which obscure view of Pagoda. RICHMOND PARK is over the hill. Former A.D.C. Governor of Tanganyika MUST SELL solid family res. Spacious drawing rm., in fashionable mud-green the whole place in House & Garden colours, dining rm. to garden which has been exposed to the ravages of 5 children. Super Kit. AGA, 5 bedrms., splendid balcony, mod. bathrm. £6,500.

ON THE SIDE OF THE ANGELS: The Ethical Union Housing Assn. which seeks *"SITE L.C.C. area for erection of building to house elderly persons with restricted means"* – and, one supposes, no hopes of future bliss. If the Ecclesiastical Commissioners, or any other benevolent body or private person can provide please tel? ROY BROOKS.

CHEAP FLAT, WESTMINSTER, S.W.1. Higher Civil Servant's 4th flr. (No lift) MANSION FLAT (panoramic vista Abbey, Big Ben & that new erection on the Embankment) which, since he was loaned to N.A.T.O. in Paris; he now has 5 children & has now outgrown. Spacious drawing rm., 3 gd. bedrms., bathrm., big kit.-dining rm. (As the lower classes edge away from the kitchen range into separate dining rms. with lit-up cocktail cabinets, their betters are content to breakfast with the Bendix.) Pres. lse. to Jan. '64, said renewable. ONLY £262 p.a. INC. CON. HOT WATER, CENTRAL HEATING & rates. V. mod. fig. inc. f. & f.

WE HAVE BEEN PROMISED ANOTHER EARLY VIC. 6 RM. CHELSEA HOUSE. Whilst not wishing to gloss over its slum-like qualities we ought to mention that our clients will only sell to a person with the taste & means to restore it properly. A foul little garden at the back. ONLY £6,500. Lse. 40 yrs. G.R. abt. £50. In the absence of an enlightened Government which could build better, unsubsidised houses for £2,500, you are unlikely to get anything better.

£990 FASHIONABLE CHELSEA. A dreadful working-class terrace house of sinister aspect in one of the meaner streets at the bitter end of CHEYNE WALK in the grimy ambit of LOTS RD. POWER STN. Time and decay have not softened the hideous aspect of this typical example of Victorian speculative building. 6 rms., kit. (generations of women have looked out, over the shallow sink with its one cold tap, slap onto the crumbling, claustrophobic backyard and outside lav.). The Master bedrm. has had its door torn off at the hinges, several windows have been broken, what is left of the paintwork is in a nasty, dirty shade of green and the wallpaper hangs dankly down in shreds – otherwise there's probably not much wrong, as people have been living in it up to now. The gaping holes gnawed at the edges in the basement flr. may not have been done by rats, but merely large mice. Lse. 17 yrs. G.R. abt. £10. View Sun. The door swings open in the wind: Stadium Street, S.W.10.

FASHIONABLE KNIGHTSBRIDGE. Rich electrician bought this period res. to extend his gracious living next door, has cut off this 1st flr. FLAT with own street door & has lavishly reconstructed it to the same standards as his own & to tell the truth, not in bad taste. Simply crawling with electric plugs. Attractive drawing rm., gd. dble. bedrm., luxury bath-dressing rm. with shower. Gd. well fit. kit. big enough to eat in. Lse. 12 yrs. ONLY £100 p.a. £5,750, but a lower price wedded to a higher rent cld. be arranged to marry in with a buyer's expense account. After all there is something rather sacred about the preservation of money over other merely material considerations.

1ST. FLOOR SUNNY SOUTH FLAT. KENSINGTON PARK GARDENS. Overlooking & access to 7 acres of private gardens. The magnificent home of lady opera singer & former agricultural worker. The impressive & gorgeously comfortable 22ft. × 20ft. drawing rm., with sun bathing balcony, HUGE 20ft. double bedrm. with sort of Romeo & Juliet balcony, mod. b. & k. The decor strikes a high note. Lse. 5 yrs. from last quarter. ONLY £340 p.a. This impulsive couple will probably accept a miserably low fig. for f. & f. from a deserving case.

WANTED: UGLY HOUSES FOR POOR PEOPLE ALSO SMART BEAUTIFUL HOUSES & FLATS FOR THE THOUSANDS & THOUSANDS OF OUR RICH APPLICANTS WHOSE FORTUNES ARE UNTOUCHED BY THE FREEZE. ROY BROOKS.

LABOUR SAVING CASTLE: The lucky buyer of this erection dailybreading on the 7.49 (under an hour to Charing X) with R∗v∗∗ll∗ tucked in the Times knows that with *"Castle"* on his writing paper & a building 175ft high nobody can look down on him any longer. And all for the price of a suburban Villa – £4,995 FREEHOLD. Some gorgeous reception rooms 30ft high. As to bedrooms, it depends how high you want to climb. No bath, of course. Mains electricity, gas & water available. Well built & must have cost the earth even in 1810.

FASHIONABLE BLACKHEATH, SUPER SUNNY STH. ASPECT SPAN FLAT. 1st (top) flr. set in lovely woodland glade sort of gdns. with safe children's playgrnd. decently removed. Congenial professional neighbours who carry their economic serfdom lightly, altho' cut to the quick when a local P.C. referred to "Those Council flats at the Priory." Charming well proportioned drawing rm., with dining annexe, 3 bedrms., tiled bathrm., super kit., bar with high stools. Delightful decor chosen by Cordon Bleu painter bride.

RED BEARDED ARCHITECT forced thro' enormous growth of family, to emigrate to Ealing. MUST SELL cherished Period rws. off HOLLAND PARK AVE. Graceful 27ft. dble. drawing rm., 5 single bedrms. (2 cld. be converted to dble. in case anyone wanted to sleep together). Boxrm., mod. bathrm. Big dining rm.-kit. The decor? – parts of it are excellent. Good garden. BAR-GAIN: £6,500 FHLD. (A Fhld. in Kensington at under £10,000 is becoming a rarity.)

BARGAIN. FASHIONABLE CHELSEA SQUARE. Spacious semi-detached family period res. now too big for gentleman engineer whose family have left home (in a '29 Alvis, front wheel drive & elderly Rolls – thus releasing valuable parking space outside). Possible, he says, to build penthouse/studio on top. 6 bedrms., fine 31ft. 1st flr. drawing rm., balcony, dining rm., large study, 2 bathrms., plus excellent basement with own bathrm, Garden & possible garage space. All a trifle scruffy, of course, but what on earth do you expect for £23,550 FHLD.

£3,500 FREEHOLD. The airy, elegant SPAN HOUSE of England's Design Consultant of sanitary ware, lampposts & other modern conveniences: forced out by fecundity. The LARGE L-shaped double reception rm., 3 bedrms., mod. bathrm., kit. Garden with squirrel & GARAGE. TWICKENHAM, in the bucolic environs of RICHMOND OLD DEER & BUSHEY PARKS, yet quick to Piccadilly. Owner eschewing Sabbatical pistol practice will show today.

£1,950, TRY OFFER. PRINCES MEWS, W.2. (Quiet neighbours, mostly Rolls-Royces). Nr. HYDE PARK. The rather splendid MEWS COTTAGE of the director of the Co. which builds excellent mod. Council schools for 25/- a foot instead of £3. (I've always known that decent looking 4 bedrm. houses cld. be marketed for under £2,000 by these methods – but then we've never had it so good & nobody is interested in lowering prices – except the buyers). Spacious 25ft. drawing rm. leading to 15ft. dining rm., a mod. kit., 3 gd. dble. bedrms., new mod. bathrm. with latest low slung bath – for speed. Lots of gleaming new parquet. Lse. 14 yrs. (renewable). ONLY £600 p.a. Rates £40.

BUSINESS WE DON'T WANT. Houses outside London & clients who rat by using a good offer they have accepted to tempt another buyer to overbid; breaking their word & soiling our national reputation. PLEASE DON'T MAKE OUR LIFE MORE DIFFICULT by instructing us if you are not A MAN OR WOMAN OF YOUR WORD. I am getting more than a little tired of people, of apparently good standing, who accept a good offer and then *"rat"* for a pathetically few *"pieces of silver"*. I pose a question to the men which does work 7 times out of 10; but I have yet to find an epithet that one can use to a woman. My apologies to country clients & my pity for the rats – after all there is no one more difficult to get away from than yourself. ROY BROOKS.

OFF HOLLAND PARK AVENUE, KENSINGTON. MODERNISED PERIOD RESIDENCE OF VERSATILE NOUVEAU VOGUE FILM PRODUCER (from lubricants to the smart, cynical, modern English scene – vodka in the cornflakes. Spacious interesting 26ft. double drawing rm. Big eating play/workroom conveniently observed over stable door by designing girl wife from lab. sav. kit. 3 bedrms., mod. bathrm., decor in impeccable taste, a bit dirty. Sandpit, some rather nice weeds & pram shed. SACRIFICE £13,995 FREEHOLD.

RUTLAND GATE. Kensington Gore. Probably one of the most aristocratic addresses in London. Delightful, quiet, ground floor FLAT of successful Building Contractor who is going to the country to take up *"Hunting, shooting and fishing."* Vast sums expended. Attractive drawing rm. to cosy dining rm., which can be cunningly transformed into a bedroom at a moment's notice. Large bathrm. mod. kit. Pres. lse. 2½ yrs. (client says extendable). ONLY £240 p.a.

∗NTH∗NY BL∗ND'S FASHIONABLE ISLINGTON LUX. LOWER MAIS FOR THE UPPER (FINANCIAL) CLASSES. Acclaimed by National Press who, by happy coincidence, all happened to drop in the other week. Plumbed in alcohol flushes out of a fountain. Level with garden which plunges down into the rustic canal, bounded by noble, ancient trees, is the GRAND 30ft. super, super DRAWING RM. & split-level Dining area. Super fit. kit. 3 bedrms. & rm. for 4th. 3 lux. bathrms. The illusion of looking out onto the 18th Century from central heated luxury. If you only have the cash this place will give you the cachet. 90 yrs. lse. G.R. £125 SACRIFICE £28,750.

ADAM & EVE MEWS, KENSINGTON, W.8. 1st. flr. FLAT. Luxuriously appointed home of Ballet Dancer & *"Toy Barrister with a socialist conscience. Absolutely ideal for a Bachelor,"* he adds, *"'or anyone else who has lots of money & lots of personality ..."* Wide, pine panelled Hall & staircase, delightful 22ft. Drawing rm., recess bar & bookshelves. Small dining'rm. to PATIO SUNBATHING ROOF GARDEN. Smashing dble. bedrm. Lux. bathrm., BIDET, PLATE GLASS DOOR TO SHOWER. Super mod. kit. ONLY £50 p.a. Lse. $8\frac{1}{4}$ yrs. SACRIFICE £4,950. "I might" he says, "sell my fab. furniture & my country cottage – in Beds. – cheap."

FASHIONABLE CHISWICK MALL, off Pages Yard, former 17th century res. of privileged page of Duke, now STUDIO & home of charming girl fiddler & semi-abstract painter (scheduled as ancient monument). Delightful 1st. flr. drawing rm., 3 dble. bedrms., STUDIO with BOW WINDOW, dining rm.-kit., bathrm. leading down to underground press built up from Toulouse Lautrec's press & a couple of old mangles. Sparkling new white painted decor throughout. So much spent perfecting the structure it's a gift at £6,990 FHLD.

FASHIONABLE LENNOX GARDENS, CHELSEA. Retired Naval Officer, self-styled broiler king and architect sacrifices lower ground floor flat. Dble. drawing rm., dble. bedrm., mod. b. & k. Well fitted – decent taste, which is more than he claimed for his fowls ("Never eat 'em.") V. modest fig. to include f. & f. Use Garden Sq. Lse. 2 yrs. ONLY £350 p.a.

SOCIAL OUTCASTS REQUIRE ACCOMMODATION. A modest proposal. Christian Action asks us to find cheap, scruffy houses for homeless, hopeless derelict women near Railway Termini where, constantly moved on, they desperately try to sleep. No hymns or attempts to convert them to merits of Christian Capitalism, just temporary shelter, tea & bread. No *"administration expenses"* the pleasant young women run it for love. Please help: I'm less afraid of do-gooders than those who do damn all. ROY BROOKS.

DARKEST PIMLICO. A large Victorian family house, entrance flanked by pillars, pathetically waits for purchaser. The bath shrouded by thickening dust. Torn up by its roots the missing geyser leaves a gaping hole. On the Grnd. flr., folding doors open to 27ft. dble. recep. room or shut to make 2 rooms. Folding doors to 1st flr. make L reep. rm. abt. 27ft. × 18ft. A bedrm. & bathrm. 2nd. flr. 3 more bedrms. Groping in the basement, 3 rooms, our intrepid representative stumbled against an ancient brick copper: presumably the kitchen. Long 80 yrs. lse. G.R. £60 p.a. A gift at £6,990. If you are too late to secure this gem we have a twin (a much lighter house equally repulsive) next door in Sutherland Street coming on the market this week at the same price.

REPAIRING to his summer marine residence in Southern Ireland, JAMES CAMERON, the fearless foreign correspondent, offers his town residence in a FASHIONABLE CHELSEA SQ. The decor is an immaculate conception of gleaming white paint pretty well throughout. CENTRAL HEATING warms the noble fabric. The impressive 1st flr. dble. drawing rm., abt. 30ft., is both elegant & comfortable. There is a balcony where a person of standing (up to a certain weight) might appear on suitable occasions. Fine dining rm. for entertaining. The Master's study, 6 bedrms., 2 mod. bathrms., splendid hot cpds., b/kit., A sunny cheerful easily run house. Pres. lse. to Sept., 73. ONLY £200 p.a. A GIFT AT £5,990.

GROOM PL., BELGRAVIA. Quietly tucked away but within a few yards gdn. dr. to Buckingham Palace. The somewhat sumptuous Town res. of rich hush-hush ex-N.A.T.O. Diplomat who, alas, cannot himself show you the place as he has flown to Amsterdam to smell the tulips. LARGE Elegant Drawing rm. abt. 27 × 24ft., dining rm., 3 bedrms., 1 is on a different level so quite suitable for a servant (own lav & basin). mod. b. & k. FULL CENTRAL HEATING. Lots of sun. Decor good but not immaculate, but then, anyone who is anyone probably knows the place anyway. G.R. ONLY £150 Lse. to 1984. BARGAIN: £15,000 & try any, yes ANY OFFER.

BUCOLIC ESHER. Bearded advertising art director and inventor of patent plastic process for preserving poissons for pub walls and posterity must sell splendid new Architect-built (1960) det. res., surrounded by farmland. Gorgeous L-shaped 28ft × 21ft. drawing rm., small study, 4 bedrms., tiled lux. bathrm. SUPERBLY FIT. KIT. DBLE. STAINLESS SINK. OIL FIRED CENTRAL HEATING. GARAGE. EASY GARDEN, PEACE AND PRIVACY FOR ONLY £8,950 FHLD. (A bargain; the newly enriched lower middle classes pay up to £20,000 to be herded together in those ghastly Estates.)

JUST BECAUSE WE HAVE AN IN-SATIABLE DEMAND for houses in Belgravia, Chelsea & Knightsbridge it doesn't mean that we don't want houses elsewhere in London. A beekeeper in Holland Park hesitated until he saw two of our *"Sold By"* boards appear in his road. ROY BROOKS.

DOLCE VITA IN EALING. MODERN LUXURY FLAT BLOCK. A sort of hive for drones egged on by the facilities – swimming, billiards, fun & games – the pampered tenants live Eloi-like in between flitting to the executive suites. Wearing nothing (but their dark business suit, grammar school tie & bowler), tenants lie soaking up the sun on the communal lawn. Cosy drawing rm. to balcony. Dining rm./3rd. bedrm. 2 bedrms., k. & b. Lse. 3 yrs. Rent £385 p.a.

WELSH MAIDEN, descended from King Edward III & an old friend of His Majesty, makes the supreme sacrifice, & sadly parts with her MOD. LUX. BLOCK SUNNY 2nd flr. FLAT & all f. & f. – save the family sword for a mod fig. Drawing rm. with sunbathing balcony, double bedrm., mod b. & k. *"The decor's pretty awful but there's CENTRAL HEATING c.h.w., lift,"* & she says, *"The nicest porters...."* Lse. 3 yrs. Only £315 p.a.

£5,950! **THE BWANA OF BLACK-HEATH,** returning from E. African Diamond Mines, has staked a claim to the SPAN HOUSE with the LARGEST Triple-sized garden. Spacious 'L' Drawing rm., a wall of plate glass to Wistaria clad patio & garden, well fit. kit., 3 bedrms., mod. bathrm. The whole place bristles with beautiful black busts which seduces the eye from the less than perfect decor, due to subletting when in Africa: anyway it's a TERRIFIC BARGAIN. Lse. 991 yrs. G.R. £20.

FASHIONABLE PIMLICO. Early VICTORIAN TOWN HOUSE of 9 rms., 3 with pretty grim baths stuck in corner. Decorative defects include a fine growth of fungus on the wall of ground floor rear room. The first floor 27ft. drawing rm. is marred by the marble mantlepiece which has left its moorings and is sprawled across the floor. A fussy purchaser would presumably have the gaping hole in the top bedrm. ceiling – open to the sky – repaired. Lse. 80 yrs. G.R. £70. ONLY £8,650.

FASHIONABLE BLACKHEATH PARK. The Lane. One of the better SPAN HOUSES: end of only three, rural setting o'er preserved open land. Really splendid 25ft. drawing rm. floor to ceiling picture windows. Study, super fit. kit./b'fast rm., 3 bedrms., lux. bathrm., patio & walled gdn. GARAGE. Anthropologist, having completed his studies on the Span Man is going to Scotland to study Pictish Burials, leaves his OPUNTIA GIGANTICARIX (you wouldn't get this monster housebound 7ft. cactus out without a fight anyway). BARGAIN £7,990. Lse. 97 yrs. G.R. £30 p.a.

HIGH IN SYDENHAM, among trees, only a few mins. London Bridge. SUNNY GROUND FLR. FLAT. NEW BLOCK (4 yrs. old.) A fine Christian home (Mum rescues unwanted babies & daughter bans the bomb; the Church of England is less likely to fling you out for this than the Labour Party. R.E.B.) Comfortable drawing rm., 2 bedrms., mod. tiled bathrm., well fit. kit. Decor gd. Long lse. 95 yrs. G.R. ONLY £6.10. A GIFT at £3,550, even try offer.

MANY THANKS for £25 cheque (from Mr. Hamilton: gave no address) for Dr. Evans' child war victims in Saigon. Instead of scanning the moon I wish the U.S.A. would take a look at their mutilated men, women & child victims, for which no policy on earth can be a justification, and listen to what the world really thinks of them. – ROY BROOKS.

FASHIONABLE DULWICH *"A village of 2,000 Squires"* says Fred M. the well known Operatic Conductor *"you see 'em in the pub airing their ambitions, their pretty young wives left at home – it's known as the adultery belt ...."* A spacious family house, sunny & fairly soundproof *"We've had the Berlin Ensemble in the 1st flr. Music rm. & none of the neighbours complained."* Comfortable 20ft. Drawing rm. Gd. dining rm. Kit. Study or 5th bedrm., 4 other bedrms. (1 as extra nursery, kit. or genteel sublet). Mod. bathrm. Garden, apple tree & number of neglected plants. £6,490 FREEHOLD.

KNIGHTSBRIDGE FLAT of **KL*M*NI*SKI** the fashionable photographer of guided missiles, racing cars and specially selected perfectly proportioned but tiny girl models to scale for modern, mass produced sports jobs. SUNNY, QUIET 3rd. flr. (no lift). Charming drawing rm., dining rm. or 3rd. bedrm. 2 other dble. bedrms. Large, mod. bath/dressing rm. avec bidet. Big kit. SACRIFICE £2,995.

HIGHLY POLISHED RACEHORSE STARTER & EX-SUNDAY SCHOOL TEACHER'S FLAT, PARLIAMENT HILL, within panting distance of HAMPSTEAD HEATH abt. 500 yds – early morning runners pass this grnd. flr. flat – PARQUET like a skating rink & whole has completely un-English air of gleaming cleanliness. Decent drawing rm., 2 bedrms., bathrm., kit. Lse. 70½ yrs. G.R. ONLY 10 guineas. £5,400 but try any offer.

£5,950 FREEHOLD, TRY ANY OFFER! FASHIONABLE BLACKHEATH 100 yards GREENWICH PARK. Very Civil Municipal Engineer emigrated to Eccles with Socialist Schoolteacher, MUST SELL fairly mod. 1920 house. Double drawing rm., dining rm., 4 bedrms., bathrm., large kit. Garden, fruit trees, small greenhouse. PORTABLE GARAGE – take it with you on picnics – a convenience for engaged couples, or those who do not wish others to sneer at their sandwiches. MUST BE SOLD TODAY.

£2,675. Lse. to 2012. G.R. ONLY £9.10. London Editor & girl sur-tax examiner's modernised Period Cottage: Choumert Sq., an oasis of gentility in S.E.15 – 6 mins. London Bridge, an Hon. among the neighbours & easy reach Dulwich & other parks. Forced move; she needs more space for her children & he wants bigger kt. & Aga for his compost bread-making. Cosy drawing rm., 2 gd. bedrms.. mod. b. & k. Decor in decent taste but homely rather than the sort of place where they eat their cigarette ends has almost survived the onslaughts of their children. Play forecourt which some turn to garden.

KNIGHTSBRIDGE BARGAIN. The gracious ent. flr. MAISONETTE in exclusive GARDEN SQ. (access). Luxuriously dec. in a rather Frenchy manner by avant garde French actor who, turning from the plays of J. P. Sartre to plumbing, is now retiring to S. of France & must dispose, albeit, at far, far below cost. Spacious & lovely drawing rm., pale violet carpeted dining rm. or 3rd bedrm., 2 other bedrms., close carpeted bathrm., mod. kit. Costly velvet flock wallpapers. The gdn. in due season a bower of roses, fig & sycamore, looks awful at pres. Lse. 2¾ yrs. ONLY £375 p.a. (Or new 5-yr. lse. £500 p.a.)

CHOKING with what an old friend of mine, who helped to invent smokeless district heating, called *"Aerial Sewerage"* many of our applicants are too debilitated to face a long journey and prefer to grope around the centre where we URGENTLY NEED HOUSES FOR SALE (I can't imagine anyone in their right mind wanting to live in London) ROY BROOKS.

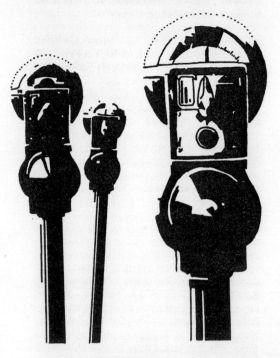

G. WEISS THE MISSILE MAN – known at Woomera as Gee Whiz (The Australians, I gather, have perfected a weapon which, after destruction of target, returns to base) now peacefully making parking meters, offers his rather fine FITZJOHNS AVE., HAMPSTEAD sunny 1st flr. flat with 4 really decent rms., b & k. Rent abt. £290 p.a. Try any reasonable offer for $6\frac{1}{2}$ yrs. lse. to incl. the chandeliers etc.

MEWS COTTAGE OFF PARK LANE, by the DORCHESTER. 2 GARAGES. 1ST Flr. flat: attractive drawing rm., dble. bedrm., mod. b. & k. Vac. poss. or top lets for £8 p.w. & 1st. flr. for £25–35 p.w. GARAGES at £9 10s. Lse. 10 yrs. from last Sep. ONLY £800 p.a. £3,990 try ANY, yes ANY offer as our client, a notable horsewoman, is champing at the bit.

FASHIONABLE CHELSEA S.W.3. Barrister & Labour candidate moving further away from his Constituency MUST SELL his NON BASE reconstructed Period House. GLEAMING NEW WHITE DECOR. 25ft. dble. drawing rm., leading to rm. for kit. (anyone eating or washing up at home wld. install sink). 4 bedrms. could get dble. bed in all. He's had all the breasts removed & CENT. HEAT RADIATORS installed throughout. He wouldn't be drawn on Labour Policy on VIETNAM but ended on an optimistic note. "The sun" he said "shines all the time on my secluded sunbathing roof garden ..." ONLY £11,995 FREEHOLD

DOLCE VITA IN HISTORIC HOUNSLOW, on the very ground worked by DICK TURPIN, important TELEVISION MAN (It's frightfully convenient for all the T.V. Studios) has created, in reality, the idealised gracious living seen in his commercials – Scandinavian woodwork & all that. A NEW ('63) end-of-ter. TOWN HOUSE with private landscaped garden (he's erected 6ft. high fences, willow, apple, pear & peach trees lawn & profusion of flowers. Fast tube etc. town. Smashing 25ft. dble. drawing rm. dining area, superfit kit. Wrighton units. 2 DBLE. Bedrms, fit. wdrbs., lux. tiled bathrm. Cedar & glass sunrm., to patio & gdn. FULL CENT. HEATING. GARAGE PLUS CARPORT. It's a bottle of Beaujolais with the steaklets & two cars if you want to count in Hounslow Society today. ONLY £6,475

£5,775 FREEHOLD TRY ANY OFFER. *"Go to Brooks, I was told by a client of yours, who said you got her £1,000 more than she expected,"* said the High Pressure (CO2) Beverage Advertising Chief. *"But as I've bought another I'll take low price for immediate sale."* Nr. STREATHAM COMMON superbly blt. just pre 1st German War but looks later, early Tudor revival, all very cosy with beamed drawing rm. with bkshelves & display cabinet & racks for the Famille Vert. *"Keatsean"* leaded light casements, beamed lounge hall with fire and seat, Gd. dining rm., kit. plus b'fast rm., 3 bedrms., bathrm., Decent gdn. with fishpond. You might take the garage where he kept his vintage Bugattis, only 11/– p.w.

CONGRATULATIONS TO MRS. BEAVER who, impervious to snow and ice, made the round trip from Brighton to Muswell Hill in 12 hours last Sunday, sending us a telegram, staked first claim to the house we had advertised. More Subtopian houses for the runners-up, please. ROY BROOKS.

YOUNG MRS. DOUCH THE DOCTOR'S WIFE (*"I'm frequently taken for the au pair girl"*) enthusiastically recommends her cheerful, superbly modernised Victorian **EALING FAMILY HOUSE** to anyone like herself with 5 children under 6½. Lovely ground floor nursery with own bathrm. Magnificent 25ft. family dining rm.-kit. AGA. Quiet comfortable withdrawing rm. 1st flr. 3 dble. & 1 single bedrm. Mod. bathrm. 2nd. flr. more bedrms. & kitchenette. Decor as reasonable as you could expect with 5 happy children. LARGE GARDEN. GARAGE. A GIFT AT £10,995 FREEHOLD.

INDUSTRIAL FASHION BOOT TYCOON'S ELEGANT NEW ('64) TEDDINGTON TOWN HOUSE. Sailing & Tely Studios? Ent. Hall, clkrm., delightful lge. drawing rm. Italian marble chimney piece., 3 gd. bedrms., well fit. kit. 21ft. garage takes Bugatti Royale or Phantom V. Garden. ONLY £6,575 FREEHOLD.

N∗CH∗L∗S T∗M∗L∗N, Editor of TOWN & President of the Society for the discouragement of Public Relations, modestly describes his FASHIONABLE GREENWICH WM. & Mary house & decor as: *"Gorgeous, superb, lavish . . . . . the magnificent new CENTRAL HEATING enables the fireplaces to be converted to hi-fi . . . . Most splendid large drawing rm. French windows to the garden of 100 ripening peaches, figs which arrive at comparative maturity & vine heavy with the sweetening grape, apples & lawn for baby croquet."* The dining rm. is not bad either. *"Fabulous kit."* Vast prowling study or playroom of *"Athletic"* proportions (33½ft), 4 principal bedrms., mod. bathrm., PLUS top FLAT 2 gd. rms., own b. & k. N.T. thinks would suit rich young couple over span of their childbearing in healthy verdant surroundings. 9 mins. London Bridge. Lse. 14 yrs. ONLY £600 p.a. SACRIFICE £6,995. Permitted genteel subletting cld. reduce total liability to £300 p.a. Might sell FREEHOLD.

Nich. killed in Vietnam = Claire, d of Emile Delavenay

£2,450 FREEHOLD. PIERS HAGGARD sacrifices humble cottage 'twixt Battersea Pk. & Clapham Common as, after working on Beckett, Rookery Nook, Genet's The Blacks and other Masters of modern drama, he has turned his back on London (*"Blast"* said one of his great uncle's heroes; *"the first time he had used strong language in front of a lady."* – I wonder what he would have made of Genet?) Drawing rm., 2 bedrms., mod. b. & k. Garden: a small wilderness.

APOLOGIES TO THOSE EARLY CALLERS who failed to contact Client who failed to tell Hotel operator: now frantic has slashed price £1,000. THAMES DITTON. Smell of country, 30 mins. Waterloo. Another of that ambient Monarch Henry VIIIth's Hunting Lodges where, it is said, he kept a mistress. (Live in a suburb where everyone knows your business). Refaced, probably in Queen Anne's time. Vast sums spent. Charming drawing rm., gd. dining rm., utility rm., 3 best bedrms. plus bedsit for dwarf. mod. b. & k. Historically named ROSEWOOD HOUSE. The lovely gdn. breeds a gorgeous profusion of roses, peaches and gooseberries. DOUBLE GARAGE. Sacrifice £5,990 FHLD. A det. modernised staff cottage: 3 rms. new b. & k. ONLY £3,550.

10 PEOPLE WANTED LAST WEEK'S KENTISH TOWN HOUSE, one of the disappointed nine left the office in tears. RE-PLACEMENTS URGENTLY WANTED, however scruffy, as long as it's under £10,000. (We still have plenty of demand for decent £20,000 houses, but these applicants keep more cheerful). Usual scale commission. ROY BROOKS.

£6,500 FREEHOLD. MISS WHITTING-TON & HER CAT (The long-tailed Barge variety which swims) offer their family home, since 1910. A fine solid Victorian family home. Ent. hall, a rather nice staircase with sweeping curved bannister, down which this charming scion of an ancient lineage used to slide *"girls of my generation were silly until they were forty .... we used to have a governess, cook, between maid & under-maid & a weekly washerwoman. MILLER the butcher's sheep grazed on the nearby common, BAD-COCK the Postmaster-General lived in the middle of the road where he had the pillar box erected outside his gate."* The road only really began to go down when LLOYD GEORGE came to live in it. Comfortable drawing rm., dining rm., drs. to garden, b'fastrm. leading to kit., 5 bedrms. (4 DOUBLE), period bathrm., admirable store rms. & wine cellar. 90 ft. garden.

43

"THEATRICAL RATHER THAN CAMP" says Management Consultant who, since he moved in with working model has become overwhelmed by the population explosion & MUST SELL, THIS ELEGANT GROSVENOR CRES. MEWS. BELGRAVIA COTTAGE. Hidden, only abt. 50 yds. Hyde Park Corner, exclusive (only the best people are let in by the attendant at the gate). He says *"Neighbours are all film Stars, Models – or Chauffeurs."* Pleasant hall, charming dining rm., 3 bedrms., mod. bathrm., well fit. kit. Everything, including the occupants, is immaculate. Lse. 13½ yrs. ONLY £400 p.a. BARGAIN: £7,995.

£4,995 FREEHOLD. WELL KNOWN ACTOR R*B*RT BR*CKM*N speaking from his London home of his Liverpool Premiers – & the music teacher in C. P. SNOW'S The Affair, informs us that, after his sojourn at THE MERMAID has decided to divide his time between his 3-acre farm in Suffolk : a pied-a-terre (he is now distributing Playboy Magazine) – thereby relinquishing this TOWN RES. – best part of BATTERSEA – nearer the Park than the Gas Works. A Nolan Henry Moore & Modigliani embellish the pine pannelling of the 25ft. split-level drawing rm., bedrm accom. comprises: The master's bedrm., a nursery & the ex-au-pair girl's room. mod. bathrm., American kit. by Heals. Cheerfully crawling with children, there is no immaculate conception and the gdn. is a patch of flattened earth – but what on earth do you expect for the price?

WILL NO ONE BUY THIS POOR OLD HOUSE? Empty, miserable & racked by the District trains that pass at the end of its tiny, overgrown & possibly in very good shape back gdn. Now arranged as VACANT SPACIOUS S/c MAISONNETTES. Enormously rich owner is not really interested in money as long as we find someone sympathetic for this BARON'S COURT gem. He is only asking £8,250 FREEHOLD.

£5,975 FREEHOLD – try any offer. OFF SOUTHSIDE, CLAPHAM COMMON. With art nouveau raising its sinister sinuous head, this fin de siecle erection should command respect. This all too solidly built family house spacious 25ft. dble drawing rm., b'fast rm. to garden (3 apple trees) 5 bedrms., bathrm. & kit.

BUILDING SITE. Worthy Charity has spare lump of land with permissions to erect superior gentleman's res. When, despite sign-posting, you finally motor up out of the hell that is S.E. London, It's nice to see the green verges &, perched up here in BICKLEY, surrounded by wooded hills, it's odd that you're only 25 mins. from town by train. We don't, of course, charge commission for this sort of job, so you'll get it net. – ROY BROOKS.

HOUSEBOAT SUPER PRIVATE MOOR-INGS, RICHMOND ON THAMES. LITTLE EX-WREN fell in love with this sleek, spacious 70ft. Motor Torpedo Boat. *"I think it was build end of the war so hasn't killed anyone . . ."* sons now gone ashore so MUST SELL. 50 knots claimed before Rolls engine removed. Claimed one of the best conversions. Ent. hall, SUN LOUNGE, fine Dining Salon, cocktail bar. Well fit. galley, stainless steel sink. 3 good cabin bedrms. SACRIFICE £2,850 & TRY ANY OFFER. Inc. all the super fit. furniture, suitable refined pop singer, Film or telly Star – or anyone like to be thought one. (Convenient TWICKENHAM STUDIOS.)

GIRL COWBOY EDITRESS & PRO'S FASHIONABLE BARNES WHITE PERIOD COTTAGE. A bucolic life – swimming in the river, 2 mins. away & romping on common – all a few mins. W. End by car (in the middle of the night) 25ft. open plan drawing rm., library, whole wall of super pine bookshelves. 2 bedrms., mod. bathrm., well fit. kit. Decor good. Garden SACRIFICE £6,275 FHLD.

**REACTING AGAINST THE DULL UTIL-
ITY OF MODERN PRESCRIPTIONS**
(stick the dosage over the proprietary label).
Vintage apothecary treasured ancient Adler
in garage of NEW ('64) LUX. TOWN
HOUSE, S.E. 19 near wooded embraced
CRYSTAL PALACE. Dble. Drawing rm., 3
bedrms., mod. bathrm., well fit. kit. Garden.
FREEHOLD £6,895.

**THE FASHIONABLE BLACKHEATH
GEORGIAN TEA-CADDY HOUSE** of
Dr. X, a successful Arborfield apprentice
now in rubber goods and French mistress
(secondary mod.) Detached dble. fronted.
30ft. dble. drawing rm. fine large Dining rm.
leading to well fit. kit. 6 bedrms., 4 dble.,
bathrm. PLUS s/c semi-basement flat of 2
large rooms b. & k. Gorgeous big garden
onto playing fields. £15,750 FREEHOLD.

FASHIONABLE CHELSEA. A clapped
out EARLY VICTORIAN VILLA. Semi-
detached so you can get your motorbike
round to the dirty patch of weeds which
passes for a garden. 27ft. double drawing
rm., Dining rm. & dreadful basement kit. 3
bedrms. & room for a bathrm. if desired.
Dirty, dark brown varnished woodwork dat-
ing back to the General Strike: Peeling wallpaper & plaster work (need redecorating).
Look out for "Merulious Lacrymans." Quiet
backwater abutting hospital laundry. Lse. 51
yrs. G.R. £80 p.a. Bargain £8,950.

POSH KINGSTON HILL, graced by
many famous & illustrious people, H.M.
Queen Victoria hunted the stags & H.M.
King Farouk spent part of his boyhood here.
A perfectly splendid 2nd (top) flr. FLAT:
gorgeous panorama over Richmond Park,
directly behind. Converted mansion, but
MAGNIFICENT 25ft. Scandinavian style
DRAWING RM. (6 big windows) newly
built on. 3 bedrms. mod. bathrm., new kit.
Dec. in exquisite taste by Grammar School
anti-Monarchical Conservative Avant garde
Architect, who must flog it quick. GARAGE
inc. Use $\frac{1}{4}$ acre Garden. Sacrifice £4,750 try
any offer. Lse. 97 yrs., G.R. ONLY £25.

IT'S THE PEOPLE NOT THE PROPERTIES who make life interesting. In '63 little blond actress & singer, Bloomsbury born, blue eyed beauty from the Israeli army (as bright as her great-uncle who collaborated with Curé) but *"had some bother with my bomb throwing – who hasn't . . . ."* came to see me for a flat. This week, on the sleeve of her hauntingly beautiful LP "AVIVA" BENNY GREEN writes *"ROY BROOKS who is as ruthless in his assessment of women as he is of houses,"* says "if she was a house I could sell her at once . . . like a Marx brother only better looking." If you missed her singing on television ask for the disc. No commission required. ROY BROOKS.

IMPORTANT YOUNG GENTLEMAN (he tells me he appeared with his mum – a Mme. Vicani, on This Is Your Life) going to New York in connection with new glamour mag. for Men – PLAYBOY – and must part with 7th flr. MOD. BLOCK FLAT. Fairly spacious recep. rm., 2 bedrms., mod. tiled b. & k. CENT. HEAT. c.h.w. lift. Lse. 7 yrs. from last Sept. ONLY £325 p.a.

PERRY GUINESS IS GOOD FOR YOU. Unable to face another 22 yrs. of well paid (for the B.B.C.) security with the Corps., he is emigrating to Australia & MUST QUICKLY SELL all that taste, money & great comfort can provide in the shape of this exceptional REGENCY HOUSE o'er the canal in FASHIONABLE ISLINGTON. Entirely sep., s/c base. flat let to impeccable air pilot 12 gns. p.w. (but poss. if req.) Ent. Hall, clkrm., the casual elegance of a genuine upper-class drawing rm. (25ft.) 3 dble bedrms., fit. wdrbs., mod. bathr., even a rail to warm the towels. Well fit. kit., stainless unit. CENTRAL HEATING, electric NOT Gas which after 160 yrs. of public supply still has its teething troubles. Decor, of course, excellent. £13,995 FREEHOLD.

COMING UP CAMBERWELL. Hid, Casbah-like behind a black door in a high wall in LOVE WALK is the SUPER MOD. DETACHED HOUSE blt. 4 yrs. ago by a brace of young ARCHITECTS (she beautified the new City of London Public Cleansing Depot). Now with 4 babies they've had to build a larger erection & MUST SELL this one sequestered in charming walled garden. with ancient mulberry tree. Ent. Hall, TEAK PARQUET, really lovely 24ft drawing rm., MAPLE Flr., DBLE GLAZING, Westmoreland slate hearth, serving unit, dining rm. or 4th bedrm., 3 bedrms., DEEP fit. wdrbs. fit. basin, mod. bathrm., ONLY £9,450 FREEHOLD.

DISTINGUISHED ARCHITECT has created, without regard to expense, a HAMPSTEAD RES. of almost Babylonian luxury for client whom, he writes *"Industrial Consultant .... got involved with a woman ... must sell ..."* A gorgeous spacious drawing rm. lined with rare woods (even the Architect can't identify them) with pool and fountain which is shared with the *"exciting patio/garden"*, the fish come in to be fed – or eaten. Study or contemplation rm. (there is a vast wall mirror). Marble paved sun rm. with exotic decor. American kit., waste disposer. Clkrm., 3 bedrms., lux. master bath/dressing rm. 2nd. bathrm. GARAGE. A bold mosaic and beaten copper sun gloats over all this extravagance. SACRIFICE BELOW COST £13,995 and try any offer. Lse. to 1996.

THE TRAGEDY OF THE WORKING CLASSES IS THE POVERTY OF THEIR DESIRES said KEIR HARDIE. I, too, have remarked their diffidence in bringing me their suburban houses of, say, £4,000 to £5,000 because they thought we dealt with *"posh"* people. This is not so. As a socialist I make only one distinction: that is between those who are honest – & those who are not: & with whom we prefer not to deal. ROY BROOKS.

£4,675, FREEHOLD TRY OFFER! AS-LETT ST. S.W.18 (named by an erudite Wandsworth Boro. Council after the famous essayist?) Few mins. COMMON. As two S/c FLATS. Income from ideal 1st. flr. tenants. Vac. poss. Ent. flr. flat: drawing rm., 2 bedrms., bathrm., b'fast rm., kit. labour saving GARDEN with lots of cement-set crazy paving leaving central bed for client's (tool-maker) pride & joy, a peculiar plant which blooms he says: "with big red balls – put iron filings in the soil and you can turn 'em blue."

A BEARDED PAINTER peers out from an enlarged historic SHEPHERDS COTTAGE, HAMPSTEAD HEATH, waiting to move to Mevagissey 5/6 rms., bath & kit. with sink & still life of Cornflakes by Bratby (not inc.), Scruffy, of course, but a fantastic bargain at £6,875 FHLD.

49

FASHIONABLE DULWICH VILLAGE, recent det. res. adj. Golf Course, architect blt. regardless of cost (*"Separate toilets. . . ."*) for successful Medical Consultant, who can't get off the treadmill & moving into £20,000 must sell quickly. Spacious drawing rm., gd. dining rm., comfortable study, 4 bedrms., mod. bath., shower, magnificent large kitchen. SUPER FULLY AUTO DUCTED CENTRAL HEATING. Garden alleged ½ acre. DOUBLE GARAGE. Decor, of course, immac. 95 yrs. G.R. ONLY £30. £12,500 & try any offer.

CHEAP FLAT, Sunny side 2nd flr. new ('59) block KINGSTON-ON-THAMES where, by craning the neck, you can see this lovely stretch of river 200 yards away. Stn. (Surbiton) 20 mins. Waterloo. Comfortable drawing rm. with bay window, 2 bedrms., superb 9 ft. fit. wardrobe., mod b & k used as b'fast rm. GARAGE. Use of gdns. Venerable apothecary of the old school will, with his pestle & mortar, pill-making machine & former shorthand typist, be moving next week and we will try any offer on the low fig. of £3,850. Lse 95 yrs. G.R. ONLY £17.

£1,990! BEAUTIFUL HEDONIST OF 19 sacrifices her Town res., One of these historic XVIIIth Cent. houses in noble KENSINGTON SQ., W.8. An area made famous by Tallyrand & Pontings. Attractive double drawing rm., dining rm., 5/6 bedrms., 2 mod bathrms., mod. grnd. flr. kit., garden with LARGE LOFTY STUDIO. Pres. Lse. abt. 3 yrs. ONLY £600 p.a. I see no reason why the Crown should turf you out if you're a decent tenant.

CHEAP MAIS. WIMBLEDON PARK ROAD. S.W. 18. 3 bedrms., drawing rm., kit.-dining rm., large bathrm. Sunny 1st & 2nd flrs. Not fearfully attractive. *"The best advice I can give on this property,"* says eminent surveyor, *"is demolition."* But what on earth can one expect for £2,995? 99 yr. lse. at only £15 G.R.

CRI DE COEUR: *"Do you ever help impecunious but hard working young people?"* writes quiet educated girl from *"A rather unpleasant bed-sitter for which I am paying an extortionate rent . . . . tried sharing flat – final straw: one of the other girls abandoned latest boyfriend in my bed & row blew up when I asked him to spend rest of night on settee . . . ."* She is prepared to give services, cleaning etc. in return for something civilised at reasonable rent. Please help. ROY BROOKS.

PARKNASILLA HOUSE, FASHIONABLE DULWICH VILLAGE (Bucolic peace 12 mins. train from Victoria.) Detached, standing secluded in Edwardian splendour. 1910 steam loco steams round No. 1 gauge track in lovely $\frac{1}{4}$-acre garden. The modernised & superbly comfortable home of retired Naval Cmdr. & lady psychiatric social worker. Magnificent spacious drawing rm. thro' arch to study, gd. dining rm., 3rd. recep. rm. as library or tely rm., 7 bedrms., decent b. & k. (Top. 2nd. flr. forms sep. suite.) Vine in conservatory has 50 bunches black Hamburg grapes. BIG GARAGE: loft over. ONLY £6,265 try offer. Lse. to 82. G.R. £18.10.

£4,950. Winglet of WM. & MARY IVY HOUSE, SUNBURY ON THAMES. blt. 1692, on site of Historic CROMWELL HOUSE: seat of the EARL OF ESSEX 1511–1522. The grounds are not too awe-inspiring. You can hang your washing out & swig bottled beer under the great chestnut. 14 × 13ft. mini drawing rm., 2 bedrms., mod. b. & k. Lse. 94 yrs. G.R. ONLY £15.

OFF FASHIONABLE HOLLAND PK. AVE. The beautifully dec. Period home of Lady Potter & gifted Designer. *"Labour: but socialist, of course, rather than Gaitskell ...'* An admirable drawing rm., new grnd. flr. kit. 4 bedrms., mod. bathrm, plus abysmal basement. Ideal for anyone wanting to keep a couple of house servants: or plans to convert to a rich investment. £6,550 FHLD.

WELL DECORATED POET & SOLDIER (D.S.O. & 2 Bars &c.) and alleged female spy offer their desirable family residence off PUTNEY HILL as they are going to live in a kiln. Drawingrm. drs. to rather lovely garden, well stocked with fruits & lilies of the valley. Big study, somewhat gloomy dining rm., big warm bathrm., kit., 5 bedrms. GIFT AT £5,990 FREEHOLD.

IT USED TO BE SAID that you can judge a man by his car: but where you live is probably a better index: & what better address than S. EATON Pl., BELGRAVIA? Here, for the ridiculously low price of £2,995 you can get a theatrical tycoon's lush maisonnette with magnificent 24ft. × 18ft. drawing rm., exotic dining kit., 2 gd. dble. bedrms., mod. bathrm. & suddenly, you come across the sort of panelled discreetly-lit cocktail bar you'd find hidden in a Moscow hotel. Prs. Lse. to '75 ONLY £300 p.a.

LADY X, former showgirl, now mistress of a couple of mansions & *"a thousand shaggy beasts"* casually casts aside what she describes as: *"Rather scruffy flat over green-grocers in Westbourne Grove ..."* 1st flr. 2 bedrms. sit. rm., mod. bathrm., decently fit. kit. *"Cker, Frg. & drying Cbnet just paid for."* Pres. lse. to July '67. ONLY £382 rising to £436 p.a. SACRIFICE £3,950.

BEER MAGNATE & refined lady sculptor & former teetotaler forced moved nearer his brewery sadly leave FASHIONABLE CHELSEA & 1st. flr. maisonnette. Own sunbathing roof-gdn with *"with real artificial grass"* 1st. flr. drawingrm., 2 bedrm., mod. bathr., new kit.-dining rm. will be made. Non-rep. lse. about 4½ yrs. ONLY £50 p.a. A GIFT AT £1,990.

ONE WOMAN surprised us by saying that our advertisement had got her £4,300 more than she had paid for her house only a year before. Perhaps, like the girl The Hon. Wayland Young wrote about in Encounter, you too are sitting on a gold mine. One of these days the people of this country will come to their senses and get decent houses built for under £2,000, and then it will be too late – you will be saddled with your present dump forever. ROY BROOKS.

FASHIONABLE CHELSEA, A PRETTY LOW PERIOD HOUSE (3 floors only). Basement: 3 rms. one with shower. Grnd. flr: decent enough 25ft. dble. rm., windows both ends, another rm., study or 4th bedrm., 1st flr: 3 rooms & space for bathrm. for anyone wanting this rather bourgeois appurtenance. Decor a trifle Bohemian. Bare walls are papered with newspapers from Eastern Europe, prints, childish graffiti. Banisters are missing since I last saw the house – but then, it was a cold winter ... Force your way thru' thick undergrowth, in the tiny garden, and you come to a fig tree. Lse. 40 yrs. G.R. only £60 p.a. Bargain £6,990. Done up they make well over £10,000.

MAGNIFICENT, HISTORIC 1st FLR. FLAT in: *"The prettiest house in England. What addition to happiness could you desire? A pleasant house & garden, fine air, beautiful food, a sweet tempered young lady to ..."* wrote GENERAL WOLFE of his home; since had accolade of mention in THE QUEEN. All windows command BLACK-HEATH or GREENWICH PK. Gorgeous 22ft. drawing rm., circular bay, 3 dble. bedrms., lux. bathrm., lab. sav. kit. Lse. 48 yrs. G.R. ONLY £25. ONLY £5,950, try any offer as client taking Squadron to Singapore – pity we hand't one to send 20 yrs ago.

FASHIONABLE CHELSEA. Untouched by the swinging world of fashion an early VIC lower middle class family dwelling, which has sunk to a working class tenement (2 lousy kits. & 3 sinks.) The decaying decor lit by *"High Speed Gas."* 6 main rms. & revolting appurtenances which could be turned into bathrm. & kit. I saw a bare footed school girl (or student teacher?) sweeping filth from rusty barbed wired playground through holes in the wall into the small back garden (sic) of this house. So the first thing to do is fill in the hole. A few doors away houses sell for over £18,000 & tarted up twin houses to this one make almost double the modest £8,500 asked for this dump. Lse. 51 yrs.

A "LADY" IN OLD PUNCH DRAWING SAID *"Although I live in Balham I feel I spiritually belong in West Kensington"* de Gustibus – anyway this large Red Brick Victorian Perham Road W.14 house has been modernised and has some very decent rooms. 1st. flr. drawing rm. to balcony, dining rm., door to garden. 3 bedrms., dressing rm. or 4th bedrm., bathrm., well fit. kit. Small garden. Lse. 122 yrs. £9,990.

FASHIONABLE GREENWICH quiet backwater CROOMS HILL GROVE almost Regency Cottage. Huge Public Work Contractor reconstructed it in a masterly fashion for own occupation – today these chaps are middle class, ties instead of chokers. The decoration is in impeccable taste. Delightful open plan drawing rm., dining rm., with chatelaine space heater leading to well fit. kit. 2 dble. bedrms., lux. bathrm., sunny paved garden. FREEHOLD £8,995.

I DON'T TOUCH COUNTRY PROPERTY

but I thought some readers might be interested in HIGHAM HOUSE nr. Robertsbridge, Sussex. Home of my old friend the late Dr. Edward Moore – the only genius I have ever met; it's a modest size mansion in a very lovely park and easily kept gardens. Farmery, 53 ACRES. Gorgeous panoramic views & the sure touch of Georgian landscaping; the giant cedar planted in 1811. Easily run by a family with a decent income. I don't want any fees. ROY BROOKS.

BENEFICENT BROMLEY. Flat Bargain. High amongst the tree tops, the top (2nd flr.) Eyrie of Man from the Pru & little Milliner; enjoying the panoramic vista across London from this large detached edifice (circa 1900) – more reminiscent of Chas. Addams than Robert Adam. Clkrm., spacious drawing rm., 2 dble. bedrooms (one 24ft.), mod. bathrm., large kit., good decor – gleaming white paintwork. Own garden & Carriage drive for car (ritualistic Sunday morning public ablutions of the Jag. is a common form of worship in the suburbs). Lse. 984 yrs. G.R. £9 p.a. ONLY £3,750.

AN AIR OF GENTEEL DECAY hangs over this Nash masterpiece in Kent Terrace, REGENT'S PARK. Town residence of son of famous film star, young Dr. X, The Psychiatrist, who dismisses it with refreshing candour, rare in a vendor, *"a dull house with 3 lousy bathrooms, ... a few miserable lilies-of-the-valley in the tiny back garden, we found the dachshund carrying bone – a humerus; but we never found the rest ..."* The usual imposing 1st flr. "L" drawing rm. ample dining rm., study, abt 5 bedrms & a couple of kits. Roof for sunbathing. £300 p.a. to Oct. 63 then 21 years at ONLY £485 p.a. SACRIFICE £5,550 EVEN TRY OFFER.

ONE OF THE BIG POTS IN CHAMBER MUSIC, leader of a famous quartet, taking up suburban residence with former girl viola pupil, SACRIFICES exciting, newy-blt ('55) W.2 MEWS RES. with GARAGE for at least 3 cars. drawing rm. takes grand piano. *"Library"* with bookshelves; all of 8 feet. sq. – suit erudite dwarf. Superbly comfortable double bedrm. mod bath, shower, well fit kit. ALL beautifully light and sunny. Lse. 33 yrs. G.R. only £32 p.a. £6,900.

FLAT BARGAIN, NW11. 3 mins. Brent Stn. Northern Line. Light grnd. flr. flat of vintage anti-nazi German foresaken the fatherland for the manufacture of 9 carat gold chastity belt padlocks, until, even more divided, their war-making potential is nobbled. Decent size sit. rm., small din. rm. dble bedrm., Kit. new Crane. A gift at £2,990.

KENSINGTON CT. PLACE. W.8. Scion of distinguished ancient Liberal family (Uncle Bryant held Lambeth all his life) outgrown FABULOUS FLAT on which he has lavished thousands. Mr. D. Hicks the decorator has done a perfectly splendid job. Bookshelves contain real leather-bound books. A kind of legal air hangs abt. the vast studio-type, chandelier-lit drawing room; with gallery (for extra sleeping), Principal bedroom just takes four-poster, and 2 attic bedrooms. Air of rich luxury abt. bathroom with its interesting prints. Well fitted kit. lse. $3\frac{1}{2}$ years at only £190 p.a.

I HAVE BEEN ASKED BY A PUBLIC MAN TO FIND A HOUSE (at least 4 bedrooms) with a decent London address. As he has played cricket rather better than most and, despite rude rebuffs before fame touched him, is a good friend of England; he deserves some consideration. Can pay over £20,000 but wld. entertain cheap & scruffy for reclamation. Genuine and not too rapacious vendors please contact me. **ROY BROOKS.**

NATURE TAMED – a sort of pasturised beauty seen from the comfortable luxury of this Mod. ('37) **KINGSBURY** House through the floor to ceiling plate glass doors of the drawing rm. (Flush fit hidden cocktail cabinet) across the flower filled garden, pear, plum & apple trees, are playing fields to the rolling green belt country beyond. 3rd Generation Lady Electrologist. *"Grandmother was a guinea pig depilated by German Alchemist who passed on the craft ..."* offers lively home. Dining rm. 3rd recep. rm. or 4th big bedrm. Lux. bathrm. Super fit. kit. Superb order. £3,500 spent. **DOUBLE GARAGE. £7,995 FREEHOLD.**

FELIX FONTEYN, THE FASHIONABLE PHOTOGRAPHER of pre-stressed concrete, beautiful women and Yogi Bear dispensable drinking vessels, offers his smart S. KEN. MEWS COTTAGE WITH GARAGE (1 decent motor or 2 inferior ones), Drawing rm. with dining end, principal double bedrm., with fit. wdrbe. & exotic decor – fabric covered wall & ceiling. A 2nd. bedrm. (it has been found perfectly feasible to keep a child here. This section has been sound proofed), small mod. bathrm, with cork flr. & kit. It is possible to bask on the 25ft. SUN TERRACE. Pres. Lse. 6 yrs. from 2.5.61. ONLY £120 p.a. Try any offer: depends on what you want left.

ECCLESTON SQ. PENTHOUSE. Young English gentlewoman, fresh from Spanish Bull farm and vineyard, took this flat some months ago & unaccountably finds she prefers the climate on the Med., where she is returning. A spacious, lovely reception rm. with vast picture window (wld. make 2 rms.) leading to fine big sunbathing balcony, dble. bedrm. kit. bathrm. A glow of warmth is generated by the stairs, no lift. Use of Gdn. Sq. Lse. 80 yrs. G.R. ONLY £50. £4,700. TRY ANY OFFER.

ANCIENT 250 YR. OLD WIMBLEDON COMMON COTTAGE: Sweeping views: by 2 golf courses. Elegant drawing rm., bow windows, cosy dining rm., French windows to back yard, 2 dble. bedrms., the lux. bathrm., can only be reached through second bedrm. "No real inconvenience in the case of an attractive blonde guest" says steel wool salesman, now famous cosmetic king. Lavishly modernised & dec. BARGAIN £6,495 FHLD., even try any offer.

EXCLUSIVE INNER PARK ROAD, WIMBLEDON COMMON. Fishmonger & young gentlewoman starting life afresh in a new town (he has just had a grand clearance sale of old stock in his shop) exquisite recently Architect built LUX. RES. Elegant drawing rm. *"in a delicate shade of smoked cod fillet .... large picture window to garden just big enough for 6 pair sunbathers ...."*, 3 decent bedrms., bathrm., mod. b. & k. Lease 97 yrs. G.R. £20 p.a. Only £5,650. Try Offer.

AT A PARTY LAST NIGHT one of the busiest leading plastic surgeons said to me he would find the time (*"Give up my occasional round of golf"*) to operate free on American-bomb mutilated Vietnamese children if I could find suitable outside premises (his hospital list is 400). I'm surprised that organised Christianity and Jewry in America are powerless to stop the whole bloody business – at least the civilian bombing, but perhaps, like **PFIZER** who gave me 2,000 units of terramycin free for these kids, other Americans, inter alia, might like to help save completely innocent, hideously disfigured children from a life of living hell. With this on our mind how can we celebrate Christmas and hope for a happy new year? ROY BROOKS.

The most noble paid-for statement that ever came from a property dealer

GROUP CAPT. MOVED MUST SHIFT S.E.18 NEW (1961) HOUSE, over 400ft. Panorama, Parliament, The Abbey, St. Paul's, the Thames and the Tower. 15 min. Charing X from **BLACKHEATH** Stn. where you will rub shoulders with the cream of Suburban Society; surgeons, stockbrokers, chaps on Lloyds. Lawyers or, as an elderly aristocrat described them, his cousin tells me. *"Daily-breaders – dirty b . . . .s".* SPACIOUS 27ft. drawing rm., decent sized well-fit. kit. "Neighbours can eat in theirs." 3 bedrms., tiled bathrms. Decor v. good. Warm sunny house. Garage, garden. SACRIFICE £4,750, try any offer. Lse. 96 yrs. G.R. £15.

ANOTHER OLD CLIENT, EARL RUSSELL seeks house, anywhere LONDON, scruffy area around St. Pancras wld. do. Short lse. abt. 5 yrs. Presumably within that time either sanity or the bomb will have prevailed. With an integrity that is becoming a little old fashioned, the Earl once saw to it that we got our commission on a house when we would not otherwise have done so. Therefore the very least I can say is "No commission required & please try to help".

Did he ever use it? or is this before he tore up his card

£4,250 TRY ANY OFFER. Forced to move nearer his lab. & hush-hush work on electronic mousetrap (still on the secret list). B.Sc. of safely negative political opinions sacrifices comfortable & stately mock Tudor (1936) res. half way between Bushey & Richmond Parks (abt. 20 mins. Waterloo). Dble. drawing rm. leads to dining section making a surprisingly fine 30ft. rm. (FINE PARQUET FLR.) leading to rose gdn. & sacred gooseberry bush (strange myths still linger in the suburbs despite my old friend Dr. **st*c* Ch*ss*r). 3 bedrms., mod. tiled bathrm., lab. sav. kit. Enough CENTRAL HEATING. New decor. Long 75 yr. lse. (Fhld. avail. for a trifle).

CHEAP FLAT WITH POSH ADDRESS. A retrenching member of the Country Gentleman's Association, got as near the soil as he could when he took what is euphemistically termed *"The lower grnd. flr."* Still it is fairly light & very cosy & he has assiduously cultivated a crop of chives in a window box. Spacious dble. drawing rm., dble. bedrm., mod. bathrm., lab.-sav. kit. Well dec. in impeccable taste. Lse. 4½ yrs. ONLY £450 p.a.

BRAVE WOMAN RETURNING S. AFRICA (I warned her that under New edict you can be executed for sticking up an anti-government poster). Sacrifices her newly built, magnificent LUXURY STUDIO FLAT in most fashionable KENSINGTON, W.8 (they won't look at you unless you come from the top social, or, of course, financial brackets). Spacious "L" shaped, under floor heated Oregon pine floor. American kit. Lux. bathrm. Lse. 6 yrs. ONLY £400 p.a. Would flog whole lux. furnishings complete or not.

IF YOU BRING US A HOUSE it is not funnelled to a favoured client or speculator who will re-flog it at a profit; anything we are asked to sell is *"Thrown to the wolves"*, duplicated and sent to thousands of applicants or advertised to millions. If you are honest, prepared to pay us the scale commission, want the highest possible price as quickly as possible, then contact us. ROY BROOKS.

FASHIONABLE BUT SLIGHTLY SORDID ISLINGTON. The somewhat decayed PERIOD RES. of genuine, but beardless painter (was multi-coloured, he says – probably having used it to wipe off the brushes – he had to remove it upon matrimony). 10 rms., water, gas & elec., but, of course, no bath. Period features include some artful graining of doors (due for a smart revival any time now). GARDEN backing onto an incredible forgotten ACRE of 18th-Century countryside, whose huge forest trees show the four seasons. ONLY £5,500 FHLD., try ANY, yes ANY offer.

TELY STAR T∗RR∗NC∗ M∗RG∗N, whose Francis Drake is now a hit on American Tely, illustrating, no doubt, that we were able to lick Spain without spontaneous combustion – or Mr. Randolph Hearst. SACRIFICES his cosy HUGH ST. WESTMINSTER modernized period res. suitable for smallish couple (the rooms are not large) who, as he says: *"can shop cheaply in Vauxhall Bridge Road & flit at night in evening dress into Belgravia."* 3 dble. bedrms., drawing rm., dining rm., new 1st. flr. kit., mod. bathrm. – both need a lick of paint. PLUS s/c BASE FLAT let furnished 7 gns. p.w. Lse. 86 yrs. at £80 p.a. £9,250.

W1. Small modernised PERIOD RES. Dble. drawing rm., 3 decent enough bedrms., b. & k. (new 8 years ago). Small paved garden with flower bed. The outlook – the backside of Woolworths – might be considered a little fustian, but, good enough for our clients (HER grandpa & uncle are Peers: descended from DUCHESS OF DEVONSHIRE. HE, decent upper middle class, descended from 6 generations of Generals. STIRLING CASTLE was *"Home"*), it's probably good enough for you. £8,550 FREEHOLD.

FASHIONABLY GRIMY CHELSEA. Elegant 1st. flr. balcony FLAT: GUNTER GROVE (soon to be one way & much quieter – everything going to the right: like the Labour Party's DISCIPLINARY GROUP: pledged to expunge Socialism). Drawing rm., Adam mantel, 2 gd. bedrms., mod. b. & k. Lse. 95 yrs. G.R. £10. £4,550. Try any offer as International Handler must move quick.

CURZON PLACE, quiet cul de sac off PARK LANE. Facing Sth., luxurious bachelor apartment of bearer of a famous name (which may not be disclosed) who, having tried his hand as film extra, stockbroker, school master & tutor to a Maharajah is getting married & must sacrifice albeit at far, far below the £2,000 he has, this year, lavished on this noble Georgian Mansion's 1st flr. flat with 32ft. drawing room opening onto balcony, a charming bow window, 2 good bedrms., rich red carpeting to lux. bathrm. & lav., super-fit. kit. Lift. Pres. lse. to Sep. 1966 ONLY £850 p.a. inc. rates.

DESPERATE FILM PRODUCER, utterly homeless, seeks shelter for wife & young babe – & it looks like snowing. Consider any medium sized **LONDON HOUSE** around £7,000. ROY BROOKS.

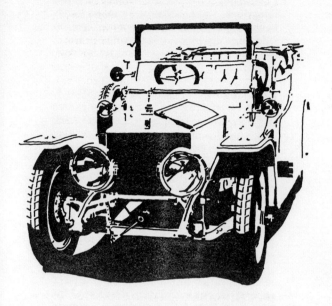

"The most sought-after address in Islington .... a title living next door and always a Rolls or Bentley in the street. No, it is NOT Balls Pond Road," said my client of his **GEORGIAN TOWN RESIDENCE** upon which he has squandered thousands of pounds and his own exquisite taste. The cocks in the guest shower room are plated with gold. The owner's bathroom is so contrived that he can carry on watching the tely. There is a magnificent entertaining room cum grand dining room, over 30ft. (striking decor a blend of mod. Swedish and Mid-West ranch house) which merges into super lux. kitchen, a Georgian drawing rm., the Master's double bedroom, (cld. divide back into 2 bedrms,) Immac new decor, full **CENTRAL HEATING.** Small garden dedicated to roses and strawberries. Conservatory. **FREEHOLD** £8,975.

CHEAP FLAT. RENT ONLY £260 p.a. The 3rd. flr., CHANDOS COURT, BUCK-INGHAM GATE, S.W.1. Flat of Mademoiselle X of Elmley Castle, formerly of N.A.T.O., so money has been poured out regardless – with little to show for it, of course. Just a couple of rooms mod. b. & k. Reasonably sunny. Decent decor & the whole thing lock, stock & barrel, furniture etc. is likely to go to the first presentable person who turns up, for far less than it cost. Lse. 3 yrs. renewable. A lift & porters at your command.

FRED FISH the guitarist's CHISWICK COACH HOUSE set in a country garden (it really is like being in the country) well modernised and converted 20ft open plan drawing rm., PARQUET, leading to dining rm., well fit kit., study/practice strumming rm., or 4th bedrm., 3 other bedrms., mod. bath. Cent. Heat. GARAGE. Sacrifice £10,975 FREEHOLD (gone to Dorset & MUST, MUST sell, try any offer.)

JOIN THE ARMY AND GET ON! Our client: Sandhurst, discount bank and finally chain store, moving to even greater affluence, offers his rather nice little 1817 REGENCY HOUSE with canopy intact, BAYSWATER W.2. 4 gd. bedrms., 3 basins – own bath to master bedrm. 2nd. mod. bathrm., charming drawing rm., dining rm. opens to childsafe courtyard. Well fit. kit. Paved gdn. Immaculate white decor. FREEHOLD £14,500.

A STERN VICTORIAN EXTERIOR MASKS the fin-de-siecle delights of RIVER COURT reputed built by a 19th cent. Sassoon for his river guests in the famous STRAWBERRY VALE. Possible to pass out of spacious elegant 22ft. drawing rm. down 160ft. GARDEN of lawn, raspberry and roses and plunge straight into the limpid waters of Thames at TWICKENHAM (OWN PRIVATE MOORINGS). Unparalleled country views across Ham Fields to Richmond Park. Arranged as spacious mais. & top (2nd. flr.) entirely S/c flat where author of Havelock Ellis has written a definitive work on the Blue Period of English Postcards. The Mais. comprises drawing rm. as above, dining rm., study, 4 bedrms., k. & 2 bathrms. The flat has 4 good rms. k. & b. FREEHOLD £15,975.

WALKING THROUGH RED SQUARE during the War, a British Diplomat told me, he wandered up behind a stranger & muttered in Russian *"Christ is risen."* The man nearly jumped out of his skin & ran away. American Christians please copy – it may save yet another Vietnamese baby being burnt to death during the festival. ROY BROOKS.

CHELSEA IS FASHIONABLE, that is why it attracts predatory business men, with their awful wives & poorer envious detractors. All being slowly poisoned by the filthy effluvia of Lots Road Power Station, the Gas Works & a strong whiff from Battersea Power Station (it was only when they found that its corrosive fumes were attacking the fabric of London's ancient buildings that they did a partial filtration). One of my friends in this road (Limerston St.) a successful but still happy architect, loves the place. *"On Saturday afternoon,"* he says, *"I take a bus to Peter Jones & stroll back looking at the shops, the pretty girls ..."*. This horror has 8 rooms, 2 thrown into one rm. about 32ft., with chimney-piece blood red painted marble & leprous yellow tiles, old shallow sink & coal fuel copper. The coal seems, recently, to have been removed from the bath itself. Upstairs the decor is fairly new, clean and in execrable taste. The oilcloth strikes a jarring note throughout. A small patch of earth behind. Lse. abt. 40 yrs. G.R. £60. ONLY £6,850. KEY OFFICE but tread with caution on the rotten basement boards.

SMART CADOGAN PLACE S.W.1.

LUXURIOUSLY RECONSTRUCTED TOWN RES. (Flr. added) Done by Architect heedless of cost in an almost frantic search for perfection. The principal bathrms. have two lav. basins set side by side in real marble, only 1 bidet but willing to install another in tandem. Magnificent drawing rm, original pine panelling. 3 bedrms., Master bedrm. with floor to ceiling sliding plate glass windows to secret courtyard. Another has its own sunbathing terrace. 2 bathrms., super fit kit. with everything down to the MOST EXPENSIVE mechanical pig. Oeil-de-boeuf to stairs. Lse. 28 yrs. ONLY £350 p.a. REDUCED FROM £16,000 TO A MERE £9,550.

FASHIONABLE CHELSEA.

Non-base PERIOD RES. in quite a fine terrace, replete with every refinement from Bidet to Tweeny Garbage-Gobbler, £3,000 recently lavished by successful & erudite Ad. Man. (*Q. "Does Wilson wearing that mac really help sales?" A. "Actually the Royal Family don't seem to wear them anymore." Q. "The Royal Family?" A. "Well – the corgis used to . . ."*) Perfectly splendid 27ft Double Drawing rm. B'fast rm. leading to lab. sav. kit., 4 bedrms., large mod. bathrm. Decor, of course, excellent. Sunbathing roof terrace, small paved garden. Lse. to '73. ONLY £500 p.a. SACRIFICE £2,990.

JAMES BOND

(alias Sean Connery) that mid-20th Cent. Mr. Standfast sort of a hero of Dr. NO asks us to sell his reconstructed MEWS COTTAGE, quiet corner ST. JOHNS WOOD. Spacious 25ft./split level drawing rm., 2 bedrms., almost a luxury bathrm. with a removable ladder to secret sunbathing roof garden. Well fit. kit. Decor bordering on good taste. GARAGE. BARGAIN £7,250 FREEHOLD. Persons carrying a folded copy of the Sunday Times/Observer will be admitted on Sunday but telephone first.

FASHIONABLE CAMPDEN HILL.

LUX. FLAT WITH LOVELY LITTLE GARDEN. Thousands spent by gentlewoman creating haven of rest after 10 yrs. cruise on husband's 80 ton luxury yacht in med. *"Seen only thro' the galley porthole . . ."* Fine spacious drawing rm., dble. bedrm., new bathrom., well fit. kit. Lots of sun. Lse. 43 yrs. G.R. £70. ONLY £4,995.

CRI DE COEUR FROM NEWPORT, MON. Redhead sculptress, trumpeter, jazz pianist & Psychologist seek Victorian house, pref. big attic, in refined neighbourhood. London area. Abt. £7,000. ROY BROOKS.

JUST WHAT YOU WOULD EXPECT the pad of Jazz Columnist on Queen to be. Top person's country seat (630ft. above sea level) built end of George IVth? Completely surrounded by own land lawns, flowers & kit. gardens, stables. SUPERB KENTISH BARN, old cottage (only 5 acres but you don't have to show visitors the boundaries). Elegant drawing rm., good dining rm., superb farmhouse style 21ft. kit. Playroom, 5 bedrms., bathrm. 3 W.C.s, study or poetry rm. Money spent like water – in splendid order. 60 mins. express London. FREEHOLD £10,990.

B.B.C. B*LL W*RSL*YS HISTORIC HENRY VIII BARGEMASTER'S HOUSE. Fashionable Thames Ditton. The one they think, who, carrying the hunchback dwarf Princess, fell mutually in love (they were sent to the tower where they lived happily ever after: producing a large family). Looks mainly Queen Anne, exquisitely modernised & decorated. 5 bedrms., fine drawing rm., over 20ft. long, enchanting white panelled dining rm., superlux b. & k. Attractive garden. £7,350 FREEHOLD.

CHATSWORTH COURT, KENSING-TON. Barrister and French girl beautician's sunny Sth. 4th flr, LUX. FLAT. (Rara avis, he's a genuine pro-the bomb Labour man. When I asked him if he would go as far as to say he supported Gaitskell, he hedged a little.) Double bedrm., decent drawing rm., lux bathrm., lab. sav. kit. Lift. Overlooking squash, tennis courts. Empty swimming pool for tenants' pleasure. 3½ yrs. lse. £250 p.a. inc. CENT. HEAT. C.H.W. to Xmas. £375 thereafter. Mod. fig. to inc. f. & f.

DARKEST PIMLICO. Seedy FAMILY HOUSE two rooms in basement, ground, 1st & 2nd floors and attic rm. on 3rd. Decor! peeling, faded and fly blown. Garden – good for Westminster – all of 20ft. Lease 80 yrs. G.R. £60 p.a. £6,950. If you are too late to secure this gem we have a spare along the road rather more derelict. A lightly built member of our staff negotiated the basement stair but our Mr. Halstead went crashing through.

CHISWICK. Leading Architect, who did the publicity of London Ctte. for Nuclear Disarmament (I hope this cranky aversion to genocide won't blight his career), taking up important provincial appointment, must sell GRAND WHITE PAINTED EDWAR-DIAN FAMILY HOUSE with its splendid 1st floor drawing rm., pale grey & pine pan-elling; gd. dining rm. extra recep. rm. as playroom, direct to garden, apple & pear trees. B'fast rm. Kit. 3 gd. bedrms., bathrm. *"Rather decrepit – or charmingly old fashioned; whichever way you look at it ..."* FREEHOLD £6,950.

YORK TER., REGENT'S PARK. Distinguished NASH res. of one who married into Royal Family. & retired Diplomat who, having ascended to Public Relations – can now afford to reside nearer his yacht. Genteel subletting to top flr. (own kit) permitted by Crown. Spacious & impressive ent. hall & fine staircase. The noble drawing rm. opens through dble. drs. to the splendid dining rm. for important receptions on the gleaming parquet. Comfortable library, 5 gd. bedrms., maid's rm., 3 bathrms, vast efficient kit., butler's pantry. Gd. 25 yr. lse. ONLY £350 p.a. SACRIFICE £8,990 to a suitable person (a reduction might be made in the case to true aristocratic poverty.)

IT HAS OFTEN SURPRISED ME how easily we can sell perfectly horrible Victorian houses in ghastly places like Penge, from £3,000 upwards. MORE PLEASE. ROY BROOKS.

£3,995 FREEHOLD. ANTIQUARIAN PROUDLY OFFERS his ghastly Peckham house. Almost innocent of plumbing, no bathrm. – bodily ablutions confined to a couple of sinks & the canal at the bottom of the garden. 8 fair sized rooms. As the artists have already moved into Peckham it is only a matter of time before they are followed by the fringe professions, Stage, Tely and Advertising – with the Chelsea type of monied intellectual snob breathing on their necks – then a dump like this will be worth well over £10,000. MOVE QUICKLY.

H.R.H. PRINCESS X is graciously pleased to flog her beautiful luxury FLAT in splendid PALACE GATE KENSINGTON, MOD BLOCK. & accept a very mod. fig. for f. & f. It is possible to make a very suitable regal entry down the spiral stair to the noble dble. reception rm. overlkg. Gdns. 2 bed-chambers, mod. tiled bathrm., kit., stainless steel sink &c. Excellent cpds. throughout. GARAGE &/OR FALLOUT SHELTER BELOW. ONLY £650 p.a.

HATCH END – THE PRIDE OF PINNER. Fashion model & Civil Engineer of those Cooling Towers that fell down (they forgot wind pressure, but no-one hurt – all at tea-break). MUST SELL FINE ARCHITECT BUILT, NEW ('63) SPACIOUS FAMILY HOUSE only 25 mins. Baker St. yet real nearby farm, where they get milk, seen from nursery. Georgian in style, it impresses all the neighbours. SUPERB 31ft. Drawing rm. to terrace & 70ft. garden, trees, fruit & flowers. 4 Dble. bedrms., 2 lux. bathrms., super fit. kit. FHLD £9,995.

REVOLUTIONARY PIANO TEACHER MUST SELL convenient S.E.6. 1924 FAMILY HOUSE. 4 bedrms. Drawing rm. takes grand piano. Gd. dining rm. 14 ft, kit. Bathrm. Garden a 78ft. paradise for children & free range guineapig, amidst a plethora of crab (jelly) & cider apples, wine making elderberries & weeds. GARAGE. REDUCED TO £5,950 FOR QUICK SALE.

£3,995. BLOSSOM-LINED PALACE GARDEN TERRACE, KENSINGTON. Campden Hill, resort of the rich. The gracious & comfortable family house of Socialist Lady Journalist & Copywriter who worked on the glowing ads. for those first cornets. (Most Ad. men sensibly don't patronise their own wares). Exterior completely redecorated: inside good. Beautiful Drawing rm., french windows over garden – French beans, elderly Hydrangea & Nasturtium. Gd. dining rm. to concealed lift to fine big B'fast rm./kit. bay window. 5 g. bedrms., 3 bathrms. Church Commissioner Lse. to 1974 (with God on your side you should get extension). ONLY £212 p.a.

HYDE PK. Off. Lux. Sunny res. London's most exclusive Mews, stiff with titles. Cobbled, overlking lovely grnds. of Royal Toxophilite Society & Tennis Courts; ideal for children – of all ages. Client tells me she nightly hears 200 yr. old Tyburn Owl hooting from her charming drawing rm., 2 bedrms., mod. bathrm., well fit. kit. Roof gdn. Gd. decor. Lse. 17 yrs. ONLY £275 p.a. Going Majorca. SACRIFICE £4,990.

WHO WILL HELP BETROTHED COUPLE? (The young man is in asphalt) who missed Clematis Cottage? Anything else in TOTTERIDGE area? Remember we can sell anything however obscure the suburb) ROY BROOKS.

RESIDENCE OF DISTINCTION. Those who knew ACACIA HOUSE only as a convent may not know that the Rev. Mother ascertaining that their Patron Saint's day coincided with the birthday of MR. SEAN CONNERY, graciously allowed him to take over. Now, with vacant possession, he must sell this fine detached great Victorian House. Secluded at end of cul-de-sac delving into the heart of ACTON PARK, W.3, it retains its air of cloistered calm, altho' the nuns' changing room is now given over to body building appliances & a bar billiards table. Enormous but elegant 'L' drawing rm., dining rm., sliding picture window to secluded walled garden, approx. 60ft. sq. Study, lab. sav. kit. Master bedrm., dressing rm., 4 other bedrms., 2 mod. bathrms., Nursery kit. or 6th bedrm. on top flr. leads to sunbathing balcony. Splendid value £14,995 FREEHOLD.

THE VERSATILE ACTOR, ∗NT∗NY J∗C∗BS, you have probably seen him on B.B.C. & Tely, has grown out of his unpresumptious HAMPSTEAD small family house. Ideal for split family living. He dwells on the first flr. with pink drawing rm., 2 bedrms & bathrm. She, a mediaevalist 3rd programme poetess, has, on the grnd. flr., a study-bedchamber with french windows to back gdn., nursery for the 3 kids, & a super kit. leading to splendid b'fast rm., all done by the chap who worked on the acclaimed Thorn Elec. Bldg. ONLY £4,975 FHLD.

FASHIONABLE FULHAM *"You think this house is beautiful – wait until you see the photographs,"* they said and, smiling from the pages of a Glossy is the Colonel (The expelled British Military Attache in Algeria) and graduate of the Rank Charm School, the progenetrix of his 3 children, posed on the stairs of their Edwardian Res., reconstructed to the highest Belgravia standards. NEW OIL CENTRAL HEATING. Elegant drawing rm. opening thro' arch to dining rm., study or playroom for soirees. 3 dble. bedrms., mod. bathrm., well fit. kit. Garden. Decor excellent. BARGAIN: ONLY £9,995.

£4,550 FREEHOLD, EVEN TRY OFFER. 40 MINS. TRAIN VICTORIA. Enchanting Georgian Village of Brompton, nr. Gillingham, Kent. Charming 1760 house with bow window. Large sum spent by lecturer of Liberal Studies, making it perfect for his midwife (Damp Course, etc), now sent to E. Anglia & MUST SELL MUCH ORIGINAL PANELLING. Drawing rm., doors could open to study or 4th bedrm. for parties, attractive b/rm. & kit. wing added in the 30s. 3 other bedrms., large bathrm. BIG DOWN-STAIRS PLAYROOM. Walled gdn. & sandpit.

RICH INVESTMENT. Lady of Title asks us to flog Ebury St., BELGRAVIA, rooming HOUSE. (1 treble, 1 single & 9 dble. rms., 3 bathrms.) *"All right,"* she says, *"as long as you don't have to live there. All you have to do is pop round once a week & collect the money (over £118) in the season. Perfect housekeeper & son do everything for £12 p.w."* £15,500 try ANY offer. Contents £1,500. Long lse. to 2004. G.R. ONLY £120.

MISS EDITH URCH has asked me to find her another big white elephant sort of house (LONDON AREA) to extend her work (voluntary & unpaid as most worth-while things are done): in 10 years she has housed & rescued over 1000 *"Unfortunates"* from lives of utter waste or crime. I would mention that as a nurse she was blitzed by a German bomb & despite permanent injury she successfully fights evil with its only antidote – good. ROY BROOKS.

LORD & LADY JESSEL (Formerly Miss de Wet *"Why do the Boers carry umbrellas ..."*) wish to sell their CHEYNE ROW, CHELSEA, TOWN HOUSE. Lord J. (Deputy Speaker, House of Lords & Mill machinery) Bai goom 'e's done a grand job – immaculate is an understatement – great wealth allied to imagination & taste have created an effect that will ravish the first American who sees it. Ent. Hall. Elegant 24ft. 1st flr. drawing rm. to balcony o'lkng Henry VIIIth's Hunting Lodge. A dining rm. that knocks those in the 'Gracious Living' tinned pea ads for six. A smashing upstairs study or 4th bedrm:, 3 dble. bedrms., a dressing rm., 3 bathrms., super lab. sav. kit. Comfortable big staff rm. or 5th bedrm. Garden tiny. GENUINE BARGAIN: £26,995 FHLD.

FASHIONABLE ST. JOHN'S WOOD.
GARDEN FLAT of LEW GARDENER of
TRIBUNE fame & MERRY ARCHARD
garden crawling with Russian Vine which a
neighbour, a Mr. Levin, said *"Threatens to
take over the whole of St. John's Wood ..."*
(As MERRY works for the Sunday Cit. the
only paper who supports the Govt. she tact-
fully refers to the growth as a Polygonum.
Attractive Drawing rm., 2 good bedrms.,
mod. bathrm. Well fit. kit. Lse. 92 yrs. G.R.
£25. ONLY £5,995.

HISTORIC MONUMENT: Grand-
daughter of Painter in Ordinary to H.M.
QUEEN VICTORIA (*"The Soul's Awaken-
ing – at least you could see what it was ..."*)
& an interesting Prima-Donna offers her
XVIIth Cent. cottage res. Enchanting with
its bow window & rounded gable. Poshest
part FASHIONABLE MARLOW, quiet
cul-de-sac with slipway. Dining rm. or study,
country sized b'fast rm. kit. Charming 1st flr.
drawing rm. 3 bedrms., fairly mod. bathrm.
Don't expect not to have to spend something
& the garden is a jungle but the price of £5,525
FREEHOLD is ridiculously low for the fabric of history & may be a bit of rot.

R*B*N B*NH*M C*RT*R the gigantic
white trader – blanket and beads – and Rho-
desian tobacco rancher returned to the old
country to make his fortune *"Printing floral
wraps for toilet paper"* and beautified this
PIMLICO PERIOD TOWN HOUSE
which, alas, his family have outgrown. Cent.
Heat. elegant 30ft. first flr. drawing rm. to
balcony, dining rm. study/5th bedrm.,
4 bedrms., 3 new bathrms, bidet, lab. sav. kit.
with b'fast bar, staff bed-sitting rm/games
rm. Tiny paved yard. Lse. 78 yrs. £18,500.

KEW GARDENS. IMPRESSIVE,
GRANDLY MODERNISED, £8–10,000
spent. Impresario & son of a sort of mini-
Diaghilev, who claims visitors say his garden
is better than KEW (Cumberland Gate opposite). As for the interior it is the perfect
exotic for the ballet dancers who flit through
the centrally heated entrance hall, large &
impressive under the chandelier. Elegant
30ft. "L" drawing rm., fine dining rm., cosy
study. 5 DOUBLE bedrms, 12 × 10ft. Dressing rm. or 6th bedrm. 2 lux. bathrms. shower
& bidet. Well fit. kit. SUN LOGGIA leading
to terrace. GARAGE. ONLY £18,990
FREEHOLD & TRY ANY OFFER.

AS THIS PAPER IS READ BY MOST INFLUENTIAL AMERICANS may I say that the British Labour Party will continue to support you even if you humanely, and sensibly, decide not to fight it out to the death in Vietnam. I know one shouldn't generalise from the particular but I keep thinking about the Vietcong librarian husband heartbreakingly separated until the peace from his English wife and child, who are in one of the homes for the homeless mums we got through this column. ROY BROOKS.

A REMARKABLE RESIDENT OF THE FASHIONABLE STRAND ON THE GREEN (CHISWICK) instructs us to sell his enchanting rose-clad cottage, snug & dry, garden wall lapped by the tide (OWN PRIVATE MOORINGS). By day the suave Dr. X – by night a powerful, half tamed gorilla-like Actor (one blacked all over as an African slave) fed by his fair wife with flesh at DRACULA BRAM STOKER'S old dining table in the elegant candle lit dining rm. Charming drawing rm. with wonderful river views, super, super kit., 4 bedrms., some murals, brilliant, witty and innocent by 13 yrs. old daughter. Mod. bathrm. shower. Cent. Heat. GARAGE Studio or extra rms. can be built over. Sacrifice £17,995.

WENDOVER COURT, FINCHLEY RD.

Sunny 2nd. flr. FLAT in MOD. BLOCK, yet already eminent residents. Plaque to C. B. Fry. (This was brought to us by a highly placed Englishman who was the first to contact Maclean & Burgess in Russia – If you see a bearded hunchback in blue-tinted spectacles viewing the flat, who straightens up before entering a black limousine, she is probably from MI5.) Decent sized panelled ent. hall. CENTRAL HEATING. dble. drs. to spacious drawing rm., ideal for receptions. Dining rm., 3 bedrms., tiled bathrm., gd.-sized kit. LIFT. 7 yrs. lse. ONLY £600 p.a. SACRIFICE far below cost; v. mod. fig. to inc. f & f.

EXCITING, STIMULATING, EALING.

Former home of Royalty & Prime Minister PERCIVAL (an old print of mine depicts him as an ass: *"Famed for doing all the drudgery & dirty work of the House ... very mild in his disposition."* But this did not, of course, prevent him being murdered.) Whilst this det. & spacious FAMILY HOUSE (circa 1900) is for a person of lower station: a solicitor, doctor or accountant, it has all the comforts peculiar to the middle classes. Mod. bathrm. with shower, well fit. kit. 6 bedrms., 5 dble. Ample drawing rm., dining rm., study. Large garden. GARAGE. ONLY £7,550 FREEHOLD & try any offer as empty & anxious.

"MAZURI SANA,"

muttered The White Settler from the Kenya Highlands when he saw & bought this shabby, spacious FAMILY HOUSE nr. FASHIONABLE BROCK GREEN & ST. PAUL'S SCHOOL. 5 admirable bedrms., drawing rm., dining rm., b'fast rm./kit. & scullery, bathrm. Garden. Pres. lse. to '75 G.R. ONLY £4 p.a. £3,350.

PROFESSOR M*S*A* BL*CK,

the famous RUSSOBRITISH architect & industrial designer's ADELPHI FLAT in the house built & lived in by ROBERT ADAM, HOOD BARRY & GOLDSWORTHY: and if they didn't mind the 76 stairs neither should you. Drawing rm., magnificent & impressive spacious with 3 floor to ceiling superb Georgian sash windows and lined with bookshelves. 3 bedrms., study or 4th bedrm., modern bathrm., Kitchen/b'fast rm. ONLY £600 p.a. incl. rates. Lse. to Dec. '70 (break at Dec. '63) Mod. fig. to include f. & f.

NO HOUSE yet in response to last week's appeal for scruffy house, pref. near Waterloo, a crude shelter for derelict female tramps who must still drag their tired sick frames from one disturbed place of rest (sic) to another. A reader from Wales writes offering to give a tenth of his income to this project. His income is £4.11.0 a week! It's a pity that our society which can still spew out millions on palaces & Ascot grandstands cannot succour those whose aggressive & acquisitive instincts – or less fortunate birth – ill-equip them to compete in our affluent society. ROY BROOKS.

ONLY £285 p.a., excl. MOD. BLOCK. V. Sunny 3rd flr. FLAT, Eaton Rise, N.W.2. Beautiful views thro' trees to distant slaughterhouse. CND Lady Drama Instructor – husband is in a museum – lavished money: now bought house & sacrifices 21 yrs. lse. Delightful drawingrm., dble. bedrm., mod. bathrm., well fit. kit. Lift, Porters, C.H. V. mod. fig. to inc. f. & f.

SHE WAS ONLY A BREWER'S DAUGHTER but, married to a Tely tycoon, has beautified this FASHIONABLE CHELSEA quiet cul-de-sac non-base. period res. He is Vice Chairman of Res. Assn. so knows all that is going on hereabouts. Elegant 1st. flr. drawing rm., study or 4th bedrm., 3 bedrms., charming dining alcove with arch, big bathrm., well equip. kit. Gd. decor. Small courtyard with plants. £13,500 FHLD. Try ANY offer.

WESTMORELAND TERRACE, WESTMINSTER, S.W.1. MOD. LUXURY ARCHITECT RES., one of four built where three stood before, so don't expect big rms; but ideal for, say, Japanese family. Owner, from N. Australia has no objection to Japs – in Pimlico. Elegant 1st. flr. "L" drawing rm., dining rm., 3 bedrms., mod. bathrm., well-fit. b'fast rm., kit., clkrm. VIEW OF RIVER from 2 rms. – just. GARAGE. A GIFT AT £10,550 FHLD.; TRY ANY OFFER.

HYDE PARK GATE – *"best address in London,"* says Advert Tycoon sweltering in his shirt sleeves & braces in the full blast of the super CENTRAL HEATING of splendid Mansion Flat decorated with the consummate taste he has displayed in promoting *"silk stockings, cosmetics & lux twin toilet tissue."* Lounge hall, noble 25ft drawing rm., 22ft dining rm., spacious kitchen, mod. sink etc., 3 splendid bedrooms, basins in 2 and fitted wardrobes, boxroom, mod. bathrm. Gleaming wood floors. Lse 5 yrs. at ONLY £450 p.a. £2,850 (to include valuable f. & f.)

GENTEEL NEW MALDEN, abt. 15 mins. Waterloo. SECLUDED IN A GORGEOUS GARDEN (We are told about ¾ acre) surrounded by trees solidly fits the stately suburban house of proprietor of Teenage Twisting Club in the heart of Soho. Spacious lounge/hall, 3 recep. rms., 5/6 bedrms., 2 bathrms., gd. kit., large studio. 2 garages. Just call Sunday after 10 a.m. Thetford Road. £10,500 FREEHOLD.

£4,975 FREEHOLD, EVEN TRY OFFER: Enchanting Professor's Cotoneaster-clad 17TH CENT. SMALL COUNTRY HOUSE, CROWBOROUGH HILL, superbly built, local sandstone, brick, oak beam ceiling. Few mins. Forest & rolling Sussex countryside, secluded behind high hedges but not isolated. 14 miles GLYNDEBOURNE. Cloakroom – red tiled floor for muddy, blood-stained hunting boots. Cosy drawing rm., inglenook & chimney corner, dining rm. also inglenook. Fine country family kit. with dining alcove. 3 bedrms., dressing rm. or small study. Mod. bathrm. 3 attics easily converted for extra children. Garden of jasmine, glorious roses & ripening apples. Not posh by stockbroker standards.

FLAT BARGAIN. Fleet Air Arm fighter pilot, now, he says, a follower of Bertrand Russell, feels call of sea again (Brighton) and must sacrifice for a purely nominal sum, incl. worthwhile f. & f. this warm and airy 2nd flr. FASHIONABLE LANCASTER GATE FLAT. Impressive 26ft drawing room, 2 bedrms. mod. b & k. CONSTANT HOT WATER. Present lse. 2 years only £525 p.a.

HER HIGHNESS GEORGINA THE MARARANEE OF COOCH BEHAR, is graciously pleased to offer to some homeless person, her splendid BELGRAVE SQ. FLAT for a nominal £10,000, including rich furnishings. To the impecunious content to live with their own sticks, the lease alone at a much lower price would be SOLD. 21 year lse. from Dec. 55. ONLY £700 p.a. inc. CENTRAL HEATING & CHW. Dining Hall, spacious drawing rm. 2 good double beds. Built in wardrobes, 2 modern bathrooms, kitchen.

ROOM AT THE TOP, Summit Way, S.E.19. Modest luxury in a new (1960) house. Level with the dome of St. Paul's – London's highest point? In the wooded environs of Crystal Palace & panoramic views to Kentish hills. Paterfamilias & ex-Met. girl & beautician turned slightly pink in the sun's actinic rays. *"I'm voting liberal next time,"* she says. Only 20 mins. Victoria. The drawing rm. opens into the dining rm. for soirees of bingo, gleam, hardwd. flrs., well fit. kit., stainless sink, 3 bedrms., fit. wdrbs., tiled bathrm. DECOR gd. Gdn. £5,550 FHLD.

BEAUTIFUL BECKENHAM. Admirable det. mod. (1954) HOUSE. Architect blt. at great cost for rich Left-wing Socialist business man. It's significant that the only effective counterpoise to the Tory and Liberal battalion is balanced on one Foot. Rural touches incl. ancient hawthorn hedge behind which is secluded lovely natural gdn. abt. ½ acre with bluebell wood, oak, ash, wild cherries & apple. 25 mins. City. Ent. Hall, mahog. flr., gorgeous 25ft. 6in "L" drawing rm., 3 gd. bedrms., mod. bathrm., superbly equipped b'fast rm. kit. Large GARAGE & workshop. BARGAIN £7,750 FHLD.

A SHABBY OLD HOUSE NR. CAMDEN TOWN that, I suppose, will come back on the market as *"A Reconstructed Period Res. nr. Regent's Park"* for at least double the £8,950 our client will accept if they like the look of you – 10 Rooms & a bathrm., GARDEN with urn. Lse. abt. 70 yrs. G.R. £80.

G.P.O. FAILED TO RE-OPEN LINE, (closed to foil Feldman's fans) in time for last Sun's ad. Try Again. CHEAP GOOD FLAT of Feldman, the famous tely script writer of ARMY GAME & BOOTSIE & SNUDGE, who somehow achieved success without sadism. PARK WEST sunny 3rd. flr. windows all round. Gorgeous 70ft. swimming pool. Delightful "L" shaped drawing rm. gd. dble. bedrm., mod. bathrm., shower. Well fit. kit. CENT HEAT. C.H.W. Lift. Lse. to March 1965. Only £420 p.a. Low price for f. & f.

LABOUR M.P., who would like to see wife occasionally, forced moved to Division Bell area & MUST SELL comfortable mod. (interwar) house GOODMAYES ILFORD ESSEX. Cosy drawing rm. good dining rm. door to 90ft. L garden. 3 bedrms., decent kit. Good decor. GARAGE. BARGAIN £5,575 FREEHOLD, EVEN TRY OFFER altho' he's had to pay this for a short lse. basement in Town!

FASHIONABLE KNIGHTSBRIDGE, by Montpelier Square, small period Film Director's smart Town house (where he conceived his 30-second masterpieces which have won awards and brought fresh delight to dogs dinners). Fine double drawing rm., dining rm., 3 bedrms, masses of fitted wardrobes, study with own lavatory (or 4th bedrm.?) 2 good mod. bathrms. kitchen, tiny garden. Oil fired Cent. Heat. FREEHOLD £19,950 – try offers.